DK
254
.L4
L42

NIAGARA COL...
OF
A.A.& T...

Y0-CMM-875

0 0 3 0 0 8 3 8 9   3/9

20.2   0792911   1994 01 25

WITHDRAWN

DK   Levine, Israel E
254   Lenin, the man who made a
L4L42   revolution

NIAGARA COLLEGE
of Applied Arts and Technology
WELLAND VALE CAMPUS
LEARNING
RESOURCE CENTRE

LENIN

The Man Who Made A Revolution

**Born: April 20, 1870
Died: January 21, 1924**

Vladimir Ilyich Ulyanov, known to the world as Lenin, turned the theory of Communism into a practical reality. As a prosperous Russian middle-class youth he was untouched by politics, but the death of his older brother at the hands of the Tsarist regime convinced him that only Communism could solve the problems of society. He dedicated his brilliant intellect, immense energy and iron will to its victory. His goal was absolute power, but his dream was freedom for mankind. He endured prison, exile in Siberia and poverty-stricken years in London and Switzerland while he worked to crush opposition to his leadership of the revolutionary movement, and in 1917 seized control of the Russian Revolution. Triumph turned to tragedy as Lenin, confined helplessly to his sickbed, watched a man he despised take charge of the state he had created. Today countless Russians yearly visit his tomb, while revolutionaries the world over study his writings and his life. Whether Lenin was an agent for good or evil remains a subject of fierce debate—but his towering importance cannot be denied.

Books by I. E. Levine

BEHIND THE SILKEN CURTAIN
The Story of Townsend Harris

CHAMPION OF WORLD PEACE
Dag Hammarskjold

CONQUEROR OF SMALLPOX
Dr. Edward Jenner

THE DISCOVERER OF INSULIN
Dr. Frederick G. Banting

ELECTRONICS PIONEER
Lee De Forest

INVENTIVE WIZARD
George Westinghouse

LENIN
The Man Who Made A Revolution

MIRACLE MAN OF PRINTING
Ottmar Mergenthaler

OLIVER CROMWELL

SPOKESMAN FOR THE FREE WORLD
Adlai E. Stevenson

YOUNG MAN IN THE WHITE HOUSE
John Fitzgerald Kennedy

LENIN

The Man Who Made A Revolution

by I. E. Levine

Julian Messner
New York

Published simultaneously in the United States and Canada by
Julian Messner, a division of Simon & Schuster, Inc.,
1 West 39 Street, New York, N.Y. 10018. All rights reserved.

Copyright, ©, 1969 by I. E. Levine

For my editor

Gertrude Blumenthal

with gratitude and esteem

Printed in the United States of America

SBN 671-32077-7 trade
671-32078-5 MCE

Library of Congress Catalog Card No. 69-12112

Contents

1. Land of the Tsars 9
2. Schooldays in Simbirsk 20
3. The Trial 29
4. Birth of a Revolutionary 39
5. Appointment in St. Petersburg 51
6. Siberian Journey 64
7. The Exile 76
8. Bolsheviks and Mensheviks 87
9. 1905 98
10. Storm Over Europe 108
11. The March Revolution 118
12. At the Finland Station 128
13. The November Revolution 137
14. Thunder on the Left 149
15. The Red Terror 162
16. Death of a Revolutionary 171

Epilogue 182
Bibliography 183
Index 185

LENIN

1.

Land of the Tsars

LATER HE WOULD call himself Lenin, but his real name was Vladimir Ilyich Ulyanov. He was born on April 20, 1870, in Simbirsk, a quiet river town in southern Russia overlooking the mighty Volga, and was named after St. Vladimir, the first Christian ruler of Russia. His father was Ilya Nikolaevich Ulyanov, an inspector of provincial schools for the Tsar's government; his mother was the former Maria Alexandrovna Blank, the daughter of a well-to-do physician. The boy Vladimir Ilyich was the second son in a family of three sons and three daughters. As a child he was blessed with all the material advantages of an upper-middle-class home.

For the father, Ilya Nikolaevich, life had not always been easy. A descendant of peasants, he was the son of a poor tailor from Astrakhan, a city in the South, where the Volga empties slowly into the Caspian Sea. He had high cheekbones, a flat nose and deep-set slanting eyes that suggested the Tartar invaders who had conquered Russia centuries before. These physical characteristics were inherited by his son Vladimir.

Orphaned at seven, Ilya Nikolaevich had worked hard to put himself through the university. A gentle, dedicated man who believed in the power of education to change people and society, he became a teacher of physics and mathematics. Although he had no family connections, his ability was recognized, and he rose in the ranks to important administrative posts. When young Vladimir Ilyich was four, his father was promoted from school inspector to director of primary schools for the entire province of Simbirsk. The new school head threw himself wholeheartedly into the task of opening up new public schools for the children of peasants who had been denied education in the past.

The mother, Maria Alexandrovna, had begun life under more favorable circumstances than her husband. Her father, Alexander Blank, was a landowner as well as a physician. He had descended from one of a number of German families that had settled on the lower Volga a century before. Stately, intelligent and well-educated, Maria Alexandrovna fell immediately in love with the young teacher from Astrakhan, Ilya Nikolaevich Ulyanov.

Within a few years of their marriage, Maria Alexandrovna had given birth to a daughter, Anna, and a son, Alexander. By 1869, when her husband was assigned to Simbirsk as the provincial inspector of schools, she was already pregnant with her third child, who would be named Vladimir Ilyich.

Simbirsk was a drowsy, unsophisticated town of forty thousand. Although it was a provincial capital, it boasted the apathy and conservatism that frequently result from isolation.

In truth it was shut off from the mainstream of Russian life. No railroad linked it with St. Petersburg, Moscow, Tsaritsyn or the other economic and cultural centers of Russia. To leave Simbirsk, one had to take a river steamer or go many miles by horse to reach a train station. Its peasants were more illiterate, its industry more underdeveloped and its roads more rutted and muddy than almost any other city on the Volga.

In spite of the shortcomings of Simbirsk itself, the surrounding countryside was a place of tranquil beauty. From the summit on which the town was situated, down to the edge of the great Volga, stretched luxuriant orchards laden with apple and cherry trees. Spring saw the hillside transformed into a sea of fragrant white blossoms. At night the air came alive with the song of nightingales.

The Ulyanov household reflected the simplicity and unruffled contentment of the town itself. Vladimir Ilyich's childhood was a secure, peaceful one, rooted in domestic routine and family harmony.

The sturdy, sprawling frame house on Moskovskaya Street was always neat and spotlessly clean. Maria Alexandrovna served her ample meals on a large table in a dining room dominated by a great copper samovar that was her pride and joy. The spacious, high-ceilinged living room boasted carved mahogany furniture, a richly ornamented Turkish rug and a huge old-fashioned grand piano. It simultaneously bespoke cozy warmth and quiet opulence.

Despite differences in their ages, all the Ulyanov brothers and sisters were close. They played together and took care of each other. Anna was six and Alexander was four when Vladimir was born. By 1878, when Vladimir was eight, Maria Alexandrovna had given birth to three more children—Olga, Dmitry and Maria. A seventh child, Nikolay, born in 1873, died when he was only a few weeks old.

Childhood years were happy, active years for the young Ulyanovs. In warm weather they fished and swam in the river or took long hikes through the hilly countryside. Winter was for skating, sliding and sleighing on the Volga's frozen surface. Occasionally, the family would travel by steamer upriver to the village of Kukushkino in the province of Kazan for a holiday on Grandfather Blank's estate.

The personalities of the children were as varied as their ages. Yet to a degree, all reflected some of the traits of each parent.

Maria Alexandrovna, normally self-effacing and good-natured, could be determined and strong-willed when the need arose. Like many Russian women, her life was devoted entirely to the welfare of her husband and children. Ilya Nikolaevich, the father, was conscientious, dedicated and completely wrapped up in his work. But when he relaxed he was gay, witty and sociable—though on rare occasions he had been known to display a quick temper.

Vladimir Ilyich inherited many of his father's personal as well as physical characteristics. Though he did not have the older Ulyanov's warm disposition, he was a lively youngster, full of unexpended energy. A born tease, he loved to play pranks on the other children. Like his father, too, he had a natural gift for scholarship and mastered his studies effortlessly. Moreover, he had his mother's stubborn determination, and once he made up his mind to do something it was hard to dissuade him. Of all the children it was Vladimir who most often had to be punished by being made to sit in the big leather chair in his father's study.

Although he was fond of all his brothers and sisters, Vladimir looked up to his brother Alexander most. Alexander was four years older than Vladimir. Unlike his younger brother, Alexander was gentle and even-tempered. A natural leader, he was scrupulously honest and fair and thus wielded a strong influence over the other children. In his dealings with people Alexander displayed a kindness and generosity that bordered on innocence. It was almost as if he were incapable of believing that human beings could be anything but good and kind to each other.

As he groped toward adolescence Vladimir increasingly fell under the sway of his older brother. They played chess, hiked and went skating together. Vladimir tried to be like Alexander in all things, but it was a hopeless task. He was far too volatile, mischievous and sharp-tongued ever to be mistaken for the gentle, even-tempered Alexander.

Their academic interests also differed. Alexander was interested in the sciences, particularly zoology. Watching his older brother conduct experiments in nature study, Vladimir, who was excellent in all subjects, at first decided to follow in the same path. But by the time he was ready for *gymnasium*, or high school, he was drawn to languages and composition. He studied Russian, Slavonic, Latin, Greek, French and German, mastering them all almost without effort. Invariably at the head of his class, he also inherited his father's love of teaching. Vladimir liked coaching the slower students in his classes and cheerfully went out of his way to help them translate difficult passages in Latin or Greek, explain a geometrical theorem or even write their compositions.

Although Vladimir was respected by the other pupils, he was too brash and critical—too much aware of his own mental superiority—to win their affection. Many considered him remote and egotistical. Thus, aside from the members of his own family, he had few close friends with whom he could exchange confidences.

When he was not with Alexander or his other brothers and sisters, he spent much of his time with books. A precocious reader, he loved the classic novels of the great Russian writers such as Pushkin, Tolstoy and Turgenev. The subtleties of language intrigued him, and he reread their works many times, seeking clues to the elements of effective writing style.

Although the winds of political change were blowing in Russia, isolated Simbirsk felt them little. Like many others in the town, the Ulyanovs were liberal conservatives who were not active in politics. Ilya Nikolaevich was guided by the notion that politics should be left to the politicians. Moreover, as a teacher, he believed that education had a more lasting influence on social conditions than the pronouncements and actions of politicians. It was this underlying belief that drove him to work hard on behalf of public education in a nation where illiteracy had mired the peasantry in poverty and despair for centuries.

Their parents' seeming lack of interest in politics was mirrored in the Ulyanov children. Neither Alexander nor Vladimir showed concern with political matters as youngsters. Occasionally, the literature of antigovernment terrorist groups would find its way to Simbirsk. Sometimes, too, there were disquieting reports that disgruntled peasants in the rural districts had burned their landlords' grainfields or houses. But such issues were rarely discussed in the Ulyanov household. Besides, the children were too wrapped up in their schoolwork and other activities to be concerned with complex political questions which even adults did not always fully understand.

Vladimir loved hiking. When Alexander wasn't around he enjoyed going off by himself for long tramps through the countryside or along the banks of the Volga. Though short, he had a muscular body and sturdy little legs that moved tirelessly, with a curious pistonlike motion.

He was especially drawn to the river. Like all Russian schoolboys, he knew the Volga was the lifeline of the Tsar's empire. This fascinated him. When he stared across the great stream toward the distant east bank, he felt a curious pride in the knowledge that he was privileged to live next to the most important of all the Russian rivers.

The Volga was the main artery of Russia. It both divided the empire into east and west and nurtured all its parts. Rising in the Valday Hills, midway between St. Petersburg and Moscow in the north, it wound its way eastward to the city of Kazan. Then, turning south, it flowed through wooded hills and great open steppes that had once echoed to the wild cries of Tartar horsemen. Leaving Simbirsk, the river ran past a score of other cities and towns. Finally, after 2,300 miles, it reached its final destination, Astrakhan, where it emptied into the Caspian Sea.

Slow, monotonous, seemingly uneventful, the course of the Volga seemed to reflect the course of Russia's history itself. The story was one of gradual, almost imperceptible change growing out of centuries of settlement and conquest by a succession of invading peoples. Some historians believe it began in the middle of the ninth century in what is now northwest Russia, where a group of Scandinavians had settled to seek trade opportunities with the Orient through the great waterways flowing to the east and the south. They found communities of farmers and herdsmen, who spoke a Slavic language, as well as wild nomadic tribes of unrecorded origin. The latter were an ever present threat to the merchants who plied the trade routes. Thus, in the year 856, the settlers sent a message to an important Viking warrior chieftain named Rurik, requesting him to give them protection. The message read: "Our land is great and abundant but there is no order in it; come and reign over us."

Rurik accepted the offer with alacrity. In addition to protecting the traders from the wild tribesmen, he and his fighters collected tribute from the Slavic farmers and taxes from the Scandinavian merchants.

Rurik was succeeded by a kinsman named Oleg, who extended the territory under his control and established the capital of Kiev farther south. Igor, the son of Rurik, who followed Oleg, continued the policy of enlarging the state and extending trade. The house of Rurik was firmly established by now as the rulers of the growing Russian state. For almost two centuries the reign passed from father to son in unbroken succession. One of the greatest of these early kings was Vladimir. Converted to Christianity, he established the Orthodox Church of Constantinople as the official church and introduced many other elements of Byzantine culture.

In 1054, with the death of Vladimir's son and successor, Yaroslov, the old system of succession ended. Uncertain as to which of his several sons should inherit the throne, Yaroslov had devised a plan whereby the state would be divided into a number of territories. Each son would reign over a separate territory as a prince.

Yaroslov's complicated system also called for the different areas to remain associated with each other in a kind of federation. Nevertheless, rivalries soon developed among the princes. Divided and weakened by internal strife, the territories once again became vulnerable targets of attack by the wild nomadic tribes that had continued to survive in outlying areas. Trade declined and economic hardship beset the people. Farmers, unable to support themselves, borrowed from the rich and agreed to work off their debts by binding themselves to the estates of the wealthy. The result was a system of serfdom or semislavery which was to hold the peasants of Russia in a vise of poverty and wretchedness for many centuries.

Undermined by a chain of mishaps, Russia became ripe for invasion. Beginning in 1223 the land was overrun by a "Golden Horde" from the Orient. For seventeen years armies of Mongols, or Tartars, swept across Russia raiding, looting and taking captives. The Tartars were ruled by Genghis Khan, and after his death they were led by his grandson Batu. Conquering areas almost at will, they captured and sacked the city of Kiev and then proceeded as far west as Vienna!

The Tartar tidal wave receded, but it left its indelible mark. Most of the Mongols returned to the east, but they continued to retain control of Russia through a system of tribute. Raiding parties were dispatched periodically to terrorize and plunder the Russians. Eventually, to spare their subjects the horror of frequent pillage and looting, the princes of the different territories established the custom of collecting tribute from their people and delivering it to the Tartar chief, or Khan.

One of the smaller territories of the divided state was Moscow, originally the site of an insignificant fortress. It was located where the major rivers and trade routes of Russia converged. Because of its strategic position, it gradually grew in importance and power.

A prince of Moscow named Ivan Kalita, to be known as Ivan I, curried favor with the Tartar leaders and asked them to proclaim him Grand Prince of All Russia. They granted his request. Fortified with the title of Grand Prince, Ivan and his descendants used diplomacy, intrigue and military pressure to reunify Russia into a single consolidated state. By the end of the fifteenth century, it was powerful enough to begin the task of breaking the Tartar hold.

The reconquest of Russia took almost half a century. It was slow, bloody work. Finally, under the cruel Ivan IV, who was to go down in history as Ivan the Terrible, the last vestiges of Tartar control were broken. As Emperor, or Tsar, of all Russia, Ivan became its absolute ruler.

The land had been dominated by the Tartars for more than three centuries. Although the military and political yoke of the East was broken, the impact of Tartar conquest was to leave a permanent imprint on Russia's ethnic and cultural heritage.

Through the centuries there had been much intermingling of peoples, ideas and customs. In many respects, Russia was now more Asian than European. For example, the tsars were more like Eastern potentates than Western monarchs in the absolute power they wielded. Many feared that European influence would undermine their own autocratic position and tried to keep Russia in virtual isolation. As a consequence, the great Renaissance period, during which the Western world gave birth to a new age of science, philosophy and artistic creativity, bypassed Russia entirely. Untouched by these influences, she remained virtually unchanged in outlook and social, political and economic development. Most of the tsars concentrated on extending Russia's borders through conquest and intrigue. They reached out and absorbed the territories to the south, as far as the Caspian Sea. Turning east, they extended control through the great northern expanse known as Siberia. By the middle of the seventeenth century, the Russian Empire had cut a wide swath through Asia to the shores of the Pacific Ocean itself. It was no longer a single nation but an amalgam of nations and peoples of many different ethnic strains—an empire almost as diverse as humanity itself.

The unyielding insistence of the tsars on retaining absolute power and the inflexible rigidity of a feudal system that denied to millions of serfs elementary human rights led to constant internal dissension. The tsars who followed Ivan the Terrible were members of the

Romanov family, descendants of Ivan's first wife. In the closing years of the seventeenth century, a Romanov named Peter I, who recognized that unless Russia was Westernized she was doomed to decline through economic isolation and military vulnerability, came to power.

In many ways, Peter—who was to go down in history as Peter the Great—was a remarkable man. Only twenty-three when he gained full monarchial power, he had already developed firm notions as to what must be done. He traveled widely in Europe to collect ideas that might be helpful in bringing Russia up to date. Nothing escaped his immense curiosity.

He banned Oriental costumes among the *boyars*—officials who were members of the aristocracy—in favor of Western-style dress and ordered them to shave off their beards. There was grumbling but in the end they complied. Peter imported Western craftsmen and advisers to teach Russians improved methods of shipbuilding, architecture, printing and other skills. The first elementary school system was established, as were the first hospital and the first medical school. Some industry, such as metal refining, textile manufacturing and papermaking, was introduced. Even coffin-making was included in the Westernization campaign.

Peter developed the first Russian navy and modernized the army with the help of his Western experts. To encourage interest in science and invention he founded the Russian Academy of Sciences.

The antiquated, inefficient system of governmental administration, modeled after Oriental and Byzantine examples, was simplified and Westernized. A Senate was set up as the supreme administrative and judicial body. All state bureaus and offices were centralized in a brand new capital which Peter ordered built. In his honor the city was named St. Petersburg.

The building of the capital represented a monumental achievement. Convinced that Russia needed a seaport looking out on western Europe, Peter chose a swampy area on the Baltic Sea which had been wrested from the Swedes. To provide foundations for the buildings, he had piles driven deep into the swamps, as in Venice, Italy.

Government officials were ordered to build their residences there under careful rules which Peter laid down. To prevent fires, all buildings were required to be made of brick or stone. He also issued a proclamation that forbade the use of stone anywhere else in Russia until St. Petersburg's needs were met.

The actual construction was done by millions of serfs who were ordered into forced labor from all corners of the empire. The work was so brutally hard and conditions in the Baltic swamps so unhealthy that thousands of workers died of overwork or disease. But Peter was not deterred by this heavy price in human misery. Because of his determination, the beautiful new city of St. Petersburg was completed in a single decade!

Peter the Great's achievement in modernizing Russia had an impact on every level of Russian society. The streamlining of government resulted in even greater centralization of political power than before. Control by the Tsar of all aspects of Russian life was now direct and virtually absolute.

The chains holding the serfs in permanent bondage were reinforced. Moreover, rigid regulations were set up governing the military and civil obligations of the rest of the population, including the aristocracy, to the state. Official directives in the name of the Tsar controlled every business and occupation, and cruel punishments were used to enforce these rules.

Thus, in spite of the Western techniques he employed, Peter the Great's basic philosophy of statesmanship remained rooted in the East, like that of so many of his forebears. He succeeded in establishing a thoroughly regimented police state whose task was to preserve for the Romanov tsars the absolute autocracy of Oriental potentates.

Yet once the barriers to the West were lowered Russia could never be the same again. Within the empire, the clash between Asian and European influences was now more intense than at any time since Russia was overrun by Genghis Khan's Mongols centuries before.

Peter the Great's efforts were continued by Catherine the Great. Originally an obscure German princess, she had married Peter III, an eccentric grandson of Peter the Great. Ambitious and completely without moral scruples, Catherine plotted against her husband and forced him off the throne less than six months after he ascended it.

Shortly afterward Peter was murdered by supporters of Catherine. Many believed that she knew of the assassination plot, but this suspicion was never proved.

As Catherine II, she became the absolute ruler of Russia and expanded many of the innovations of Peter the Great. Although Germanic in origin, she quickly became thoroughly Russian in thought and deed. Shrewd, brilliant and domineering, she extended Russia's boundaries through conquest to include large areas of Poland and portions of the coast of the Black Sea. In addition, she expanded the school system, introduced French culture to the court and aristocracy and reformed the administrative system of local and provincial governments. But she retained the traditional tsarist attitude of inflexible resistance to social and economic reforms for the peasantry.

When Catherine died in 1796, the entire world paused to take notice of the death of a remarkable and ruthless woman. But within Russia the seeds of modernization planted by Peter the Great and nurtured by Catherine had brought forth growing dissatisfaction and conflict. Windows had been opened to the West and some Russians began to peer out. Revolutions had taken place in America and France. In England and other nations of Europe, rudimentary movements were already under way to improve the lot of the poor and downtrodden. As a result, a few in Russia began to question the repression and cruelty of a caste system that represented a carry-over from an earlier, more barbaric age. It was the beginning of an era of social and political upheaval in Russia that was to last for over a century.

2.

Schooldays in Simbirsk

LIKE MOST SCHOOLBOYS, young Vladimir Ilyich Ulyanov was familiar with such facts of Russian history as the names of the tsars and when they reigned. But he was innocent of the deeper social, political and economic issues. Little wonder. His taste in reading was limited largely to language and literature. Even if he had been interested in politics he would have had access only to books that were carefully screened by the *Okhrana*, the secret police. Frank discussions of such sensitive subjects were not encouraged in the tsarist public schools.

Vladimir was thus unaware of the real implications of an event that occurred when he was almost eleven—one that jolted Russia and the world. On March 13, 1881, Tsar Alexander II was killed by a bomb thrown by three members of a terrorist group known as *Narodnaya Volya*—"The People's Will." Numerous unsuccessful terrorist attempts had been made on the Tsar's life before. Yet the knowledge that he was a constant target for assassination did not lessen the shock effect of his murder on the people of Russia. Many, including the Tsar himself, had been convinced that he was under the protection of divine providence.

Moreover, Alexander II had proved to be one of the more popular Russian rulers. Among those who mourned his passing were liberal, well-educated Russians who were concerned with social progress. During his twenty-six-year reign the Tsar had introduced some limited reforms, including the legal emancipation of the serfs, the abolition of corporal punishment and improvements in the educational system.

These reforms were due not to a revolutionary zeal on Alexander's part, but to his belief that they would calm the rising tide of discontent sweeping across Russia. Actually, the Tsar was an autocrat, not too different from his predecessors in basic outlook. But he was shrewd enough to understand that repressive tactics alone could not still a growing clamor for improved conditions for the masses.

Even the Tsar's liberal supporters conceded that he had failed to solve many of Russia's basic problems. Indeed, in some respects, the people were as badly off as they had been before. This was especially true of the peasants. While legally freeing them from their erstwhile landowner masters, the emancipation of the serfs in 1861 had enslaved them to a new owner—the *mir,* or Russian village.

The government had purchased land from the nobility so the peasants could support themselves. But these former serfs were not permitted to buy the land as private property. Instead, it was sold to the villages, to be used on a communal basis by the peasants. The mir collected redemption and tax money, enforced strict regulations and supervised the cultivation of the land just as the landowners had done earlier. Consequently, most of the peasantry were little freer now than they had been before under individual masters.

The limited reforms disappointed and angered the more radical elements. Many of them were university students. Demonstrations were organized and terrorist plots hatched, in the hope that they would trigger a full-scale revolution.

The more moderate liberals agreed that the reforms had not been far-reaching enough; but they felt that even though limited, they were an important step in the right direction. Since Alexander II had already gone beyond any tsar in history in this respect, they had felt he could be persuaded to go even further. However, now that he was gone, they feared that the progressive trend might be reversed under a less sophisticated ruler.

Ilya Ulyanov was among those who considered the assassination of Alexander to be a tragedy for Russia. Sadly, he dressed up in his official uniform and went to Simbirsk cathedral to mourn the death of the "Tsar-liberator." From his father, Vladimir sensed that the Tsar's death was a serious matter although he was too young to understand the deeper implications. But he was unable to find out whether his older brother, whose ideas he respected, also considered the murder to be an evil act, for Alexander kept his thoughts to himself.

Religion, like politics, was neither encouraged nor discouraged in the Ulyanov household. Maria Alexandrovna, who was of German Lutheran stock, did not attend church. Ilya Nikolaevich, conditioned by strong Russian Orthodox influences since childhood, was a faithful churchgoer all his life.

When they were very young, all the Ulyanov children followed their father's religion, even though Ilya did not force it on them. Then one day he noticed that Alexander had stopped going to church. The older Ulyanov asked his son if he planned to attend vespers, evening services, that night. Alexander's answer was a quiet but firm "No." Whether due to the decisive tone in the boy's voice or his own conviction that coercion had no place in spiritual matters, Ilya did not pursue the subject. Alexander never again set foot inside a church. Characteristically, he had discussed his decision with no one—not even Vladimir. Whatever spiritual conflict had taken place, he had kept within himself. Vladimir, on the other hand, remained a faithful churchgoer throughout his adolescent years.

By the time Vladimir was in his teens, his and Alexander's paths had already diverged. The differences in temperament and intellectual interests could not help but affect their relationship. Alexander grew even quieter and more introspective than before. Now he rarely confided in Vladimir as he had often done in the old days. Occasionally he showed a rare display of irritation at his younger brother's boisterous and sometimes insolent behavior. Once when Maria Alexandrovna asked Vladimir to do a household chore, he replied impertinently that he was too busy. Alexander overheard the exchange and took his brother aside. "Either you'll do what your mother tells you to do or I'll never play chess with you again!" he warned severely. Without another word, the chagrined Vladimir hurried off to do what she had asked.

As he grew older, Alexander developed an increasing concern with social issues. His basic interest was still in science, and he planned to major in biology at the university. But even isolation in a town like Simbirsk failed to shield him from the political rumblings sweeping across the land. One of the books he had managed to obtain was entitled *Capital*. The author was a German named Karl Marx. Marx had developed a revolutionary economic interpretation of history. He foresaw political movements in all countries that would topple the ruling classes and set up revolutionary governments run by the people themselves. Alexander spent many weeks studying Marx with growing fascination. Although Vladimir saw his brother reading *Capital*, which had been denounced as a "dangerous" book, he himself had no interest in the book or its subject matter. He much preferred his old favorites, the novels of Turgenev and Tolstoy.

Alexander Ulyanov's curiosity about Marx and revolutionary doctrine was shared by increasing numbers of educated young Russians. Resentment of social injustice and a need to rebel against governmental autocracy were natural outgrowths of youthful idealism. And in the Russian Empire of the 1880's there was growing cause for such resentment.

Following the assassination of Alexander II in 1881 the moderates, who had worried that the reforms begun by the dead Tsar might be curbed, found their worst fears realized. His son and successor, Tsar Alexander III, was a corpulent giant of a man who could bend an iron horseshoe with his bare hands. But he was a frightened ruler who feared the fate of his father and lacked his father's insight. The new Tsar decided that the only way to deal with discontent and would-be assassins was to restore the reign of terror of an earlier time in Russian history.

He promptly rescinded additional reforms which Alexander II had been planning at the time of his death. At the same time, he expanded the police force and enlisted armies of paid undercover agents to report on anti-Tsarist activities. Members of terrorist groups were arrested or exiled. Six were hanged. The few liberal newspapers were closed down. Libraries were "cleansed" of all books and materials deemed radical or dangerous, and rigid restrictions were placed on the professors and curricula of the universities. Restrictions on the freedom of Jews were strengthened. Even the governing powers of the *zemstvos*—the locally elected assemblies of counties and provinces—were sharply curtailed.

One of the harshest policies introduced by Alexander III was the establishment of a system of "rural chiefs." The function of these officials was to impose controls over the peasantry even beyond those exercised by the mir, or village, which held the land tilled by the peasants. Since the emancipation from serfdom had taken place only twenty-five years before, this new policy immediately reawakened bitter memories of earlier times. The "rural chief" was frighteningly reminiscent of the powerful landowners who had starved the serfs, beaten them and helped the Tsar's conscription officers locate them and drag them off to serve in the army.

While the legal emancipation of the serfs had resulted in many being worse off than before from an economic standpoint, it had at least opened up new vistas of freedom. The expansion of public schools under Alexander II—the program in which educators like Ilya Ulyanov played a key role—had given promise of a better future for the children of the masses.

The new Tsar's harsh measures dashed the hopes of those who had foreseen a new day for Russia. The job of the "rural chiefs" was to keep the peasants chained to their inferior role and discourage them from aspiring to a better life. To make sure that the lower classes would "know their place," Alexander III reversed his father's liberal educational policies. His Minister of Education issued a directive that "the children of coachmen, servants, cooks, laundresses, small shopkeepers, and suchlike should not be encouraged to rise above the sphere in which they were born."

Sensitive youths like Alexander Ulyanov were disillusioned to the point of despair. Convinced that Russia was lost as long as a despot like Tsar Alexander III occupied the throne, they took eagerly to revolutionary doctrines. Such writers as Karl Marx stirred their imagination and gave them new hope. However, if Ilya Nikolaevich was aware of his oldest son's new interest in radical political ideas, he gave no sign.

Alexander was graduated with honors from the gymnasium in

1884, when he was eighteen. It had already been agreed that he would attend the University of St. Petersburg to complete his advanced science studies. So, in the fall, his family proudly accompanied him to the railroad station in Syzran, sixty miles away, to see him off on the long seven-hundred-mile journey to the capital. Anna, the oldest Ulyanov child, was already in St. Petersburg studying to be an elementary school teacher. Just before the train pulled out, Maria Alexandrovna hugged and kissed her oldest son and reminded him once more to look up Anna. He assured her he would.

With the oldest children away, Vladimir felt lost for a time. He especially missed Alexander, even though they had not been close of late. Because of his quiet strength, the older boy's presence had provided his brothers and sisters with a sense of order and security.

Now that Alexander was gone, Vladimir's rebellious instincts found new outlets, particularly at school. Although he led his class scholastically, he frequently was insolent to the teachers. Many, he felt, were incompetent, and his attitude toward them reflected this sentiment. Complaints were finally lodged with his father by the embarrassed school principal. Vladimir was given a severe tongue-lashing by his father and warned that he must never again show disrespect to his teachers. It was one of the few times the older Ulyanov had displayed such unrestrained anger. The boy was thoroughly chastened and promised to mend his ways.

Ordinarily Ilya Nikolaevich did not allow his temper to get the better of him. But these were not ordinary times. In the spring of 1885, he had suffered a severe emotional blow.

Having completed his twenty-fifth year of service with the Ministry of Education, Ilya had been given a testimonial reception by his professional colleagues and friends. Although some school directors were retired after twenty-five years, those with good records were usually retained for five more years at full salary. There was little doubt that with his excellent record he would be asked to stay. Accordingly, he was shocked to learn that he would be kept on for only one more year. Surely there must be some mistake, he reassured his family. A letter was sent off at once to the Ministry of Education. The reply showed that there had been no mistake. He would indeed have to retire in another year! Furthermore, the Ministry letter declared coldly, the decision was irrevocable and there was no avenue of appeal.

No reasons were given, no explanation made. Ilya speculated bitterly as to why the Ministry had acted as it had. He wondered whether someone with important connections wanted his job. Or perhaps it had to do with Tsar Alexander III's program of curbing educational development. It was possible that the government did not want to keep those officials who had shown initiative in expanding the school system. Whatever the reason, it remained hidden away in confidential files.

As a sensitive man who had devoted his entire career to the Ministry of Education, Ilya was crushed. The action of the Ministry and the coldly impersonal way in which the action was taken convinced him that he had lost the confidence of his superiors. As a result, his confidence in himself was badly shaken. He grew anxious, worried and short-tempered, for he felt that he had been shamed in the eyes of his family, co-workers and friends.

Even the younger children sensed his hurt and shared his anxiety for the future. When Christmas came that year, it was not accompanied by the happy holiday atmosphere they had always known. A melancholy mood gripped the Ulyanov household. The gloom was intensified by the fact that Alexander was not with them, although his mother had written asking him to return with Anna for the holidays. With characteristic thoughtfulness, he had replied that he could not see the sense of spending money on an expensive journey home and would remain in St. Petersburg. Alexander also informed them that he had managed to save money out of the allowance they had been sending him. He had been receiving forty rubles a month (about twenty dollars) to cover all his costs. By frugal living, he found that he could get along on far less. Mr. and Mrs. Ulyanov were deeply touched. They knew that it was their son's way of trying to lighten their load in anticipation of his father's approaching retirement. Yet they were upset to think that he was living like a poor student in order to save a kopeck here and there. They felt it was unnecessary, since the money had already been set aside for his education. But in spite of their pleading, Alexander stubbornly refused to use the additional money, even for a train ticket. Anna arrived from St. Petersburg alone.

As the end of the holiday season approached, Ilya Nikolaevich grew increasingly melancholy. There were occasions when he did not seem to be himself at all. One evening, Anna was reading aloud to him in his study when he began to mutter incoherently. She asked him anxiously what was wrong, but he seemed completely unaware of her presence. Later in the evening, he appeared to have recovered completely from his brief spell. Everyone felt a sense of relief.

The next day Ilya looked worn and haggard. It was obvious that he had slept miserably, yet he did not complain. During the morning he met with several subordinates in his study and was perfectly lucid. They went over various school matters. Then, in the afternoon, he began to wear a glazed look, like that of a man in a trance.

Just before evening Maria Alexandrovna found him in his study, lying on his black leather sofa. From his facial expression and peculiar breathing she sensed that something was terribly wrong. She shouted to Vladimir and Anna to come quickly. They rushed into the study, arriving just in time to see their father die. The sight of Ilya's drawn white face and lifeless eyes impressed itself indelibly on Vladimir's consciousness. It was a memory that would remain with him all his life.

The funeral of Ilya Nikolaevich Ulyanov, who was only fifty-four at the time of his death, was one of the most important ever held in Simbirsk. His achievements in expanding the schools were not lost on the teachers under his jurisdiction and others who knew him well. People came from throughout the province to attend the elaborate Russian Orthodox funeral service. Vladimir listened to the solemn intonation of the priest and felt as if it were all a dream. He could not believe that his father would never again be with them.

Newspapers as far away as Moscow and St. Petersburg carried obituaries paying tribute to Ilya. He was described as a man of exemplary zeal and deep humanity, an educator who had been responsible for the establishment of almost five hundred new schools!

For the young Ulyanovs, pride in their father's accomplishments was obscured by grief. Maria Alexandrovna mustered all her strength to set an example of stoicism for her children. She spoke to them

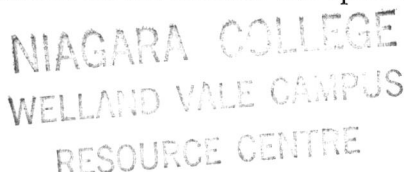

calmly, reassuring the older ones and quieting the fears of the younger.

Curiously, it was nineteen-year-old Alexander—who had arrived just in time for the funeral—who took it the hardest. The other children had looked to him for support as in the past. But instead of accepting the fact of his father's death calmly and sensibly, he reacted almost irrationally. Anna, who returned with him to St. Petersburg afterward, wrote that for days Alexander did no studying at all. He merely paced the floor of his room like a hurt, helpless child, not saying a word to anyone.

With the two oldest children away, it was fifteen-year-old Vladimir who suddenly found himself the male head of the household in Simbirsk. He assisted his mother in making family decisions, filled out the official papers for his father's pension and coaxed the younger children to return to their studies. These were responsibilities he had never faced before, yet he carried them out effectively.

Fortunately, because of his high position, Ilya's pension turned out to be substantial for those days—2,200 rubles a year, the equivalent of about $1,100. Since the family no longer needed all the rooms in the house on Moskovskaya Street, several were rented out to paying guests. There was also a regular sum coming in from Maria Alexandrovna's father's estate. Dr. Blank, who had died some years earlier, had provided that the income from the estate should be shared among his children. Thus, while the Ulyanovs could no longer afford luxuries, the money they received from all sources enabled them to live in minimal comfort.

In addition to helping run the household, Vladimir did his own lessons conscientiously and remained at the head of his class. He even managed to continue his outside tutoring activities.

The cumulative strain of his varied responsibilities was great, considering that he was only fifteen. But Vladimir did not break under them. On the contrary, he threw himself into his work with such fierce determination that his mother had to plead with him to slow down. He did not do so. Vladimir had already learned that the best way to ease his grief was to keep so busy that he would not have time to cry.

3.

The Trial

ON MARCH 13, 1887, twenty-year-old Alexander Ulyanov was arrested by the St. Petersburg police. He was one of a group of youths taken into custody for conspiring to assassinate Tsar Alexander III.

Vladimir was the first in the family to be told of his brother's arrest. He was given the shocking news by a friend of the Ulyanovs, a gray-haired Simbirsk schoolteacher named Vera Kashkadamova. She had received a letter from an acquaintance in St. Petersburg who felt that she could be depended on to inform the family as tactfully as possible. The letter indicated that Anna, too, had been picked up on suspicion because of her relationship to Alexander, although the charges against her were not nearly as serious.

Vera Kashkadamova spoke to Vladimir quietly and sympathetically. She begged him to break the news to his mother gently, pointing out that the facts were still sketchy and they should not jump to hasty conclusions. But the boy was too stunned to accept reassurance. "It's a serious matter and may turn out badly for my brother," he replied slowly, in a choked voice.

Half-dazed, he returned home and related what the schoolteacher had told him. His mother hurried off to Vera Kashkadamova's house to obtain the letter. While reading it, she began to weep. Then she regained her composure and announced determinedly that she must go to St. Petersburg at once to save her son and daughter.

For Vladimir the weeks that followed were a nightmare. Not yet seventeen, he found himself in full charge of the household and his younger brothers and sisters while his mother was away. He also had to prepare for his senior year examinations, which were only a few months off. And to add to his burden there were unpleasant community pressures to be endured, for by now everyone in Simbirsk knew of Alexander's and Anna's arrest. The Ulyanov children were well aware of the whispering and finger-pointing. Even the youngest felt the stigma of notoriety and shame.

What stung Vladimir deeply was the fact that aside from Vera Kashkadamova and one or two others, none of his father's old friends called to offer help or sympathy. He could not understand it. Just a year ago, these people had paid glowing tribute to Ilya Ulyanov at his public funeral. Yet now they shrunk away from the Ulyanov home as if it were marked by the plague. Surely friendship was not so cheap that it could be discarded so easily, he speculated bitterly.

Through letters from his mother in St. Petersburg, Vladimir learned more of the details of the arrest. Unfortunately, they tended to bear out his earlier fears that the charges were grave indeed, particularly those against his brother.

It had all begun the previous September when Alexander returned to school after the summer vacation. Until that time, he had played no part in political activities at the university. He had read Karl Marx, it was true, but his interest in revolution had been purely theoretical and intellectual. No one suspected that Alexander Ulyanov, the quiet, gentle honor student in science, could ever participate in a terrorist scheme to kill the Tsar.

In the fall he began to participate for the first time in student demonstrations. These were peaceful, orderly assemblages designed to pay homage to the memory of Russian officials and thinkers who had brought about reforms during the reign of Alexander II. One such meeting was broken up by a cordon of police, and forty students were discharged from St. Petersburg University.

Alexander was not one of those expelled. Nevertheless, he protested the university's action by helping to distribute leaflets denouncing restrictions on student freedom. When these handbills were confiscated by the police, he and others were convinced that all legitimate avenues of protest had been closed off. Now they must resort to more violent measures. . . .

Violence was hardly alien to Russian political life. It was almost as much a part of the national heritage as the absolute powers of the Tsar himself. In fact, these two characteristics—violence and absolutism—were related. The traditional violence and cruelty of the Russian despots had set a pattern that was emulated by many of those seeking to end tsarist oppression.

Ever since the development of serfdom there had been occasional revolts against the government. Some of these had been carefully planned and led. At other times, unorganized mobs of peasants would simply attack large estates, burn their landlords' houses and murder the occupants.

One of the best-known revolts took place during the reign of Catherine the Great. Its leader, Emilian Pugachev, was an illiterate peasant-turned-soldier from southern Russia. The uprising began among the Cossacks, famed Russian horsemen who traditionally served as mounted troops charged with policing the empire's frontiers. Pugachev was cunning and resourceful enough to persuade thousands of dissatisfied peasants to join the Cossack revolt by exploiting their superstitious nature. Claiming to be Peter III, the murdered husband of Catherine the Great, he promised to overthrow the landlords, drive Catherine from the throne and divide the land among the peasants. At times his ragtag serf army numbered more than thirty thousand. They killed and looted over a wide area, causing deep concern and fear among the Russian nobility.

Pugachev was finally defeated by Catherine's soldiers, taken prisoner and beheaded. But among the oppressed he became a legend— a sort of Slavic Robin Hood who had used violence to fight the violence of the ruling classes.

In the decades that followed, popular discontent grew and revolts became more frequent. During the early 1800's, following the defeat of Napoleon, many young Russian officers were stationed in western Europe where they were exposed to new ideas. Some were deeply concerned with the backwardness of their nation's political, economic and social development. When they returned to Russia, they began to establish secret societies to fight for reform. Most wanted to replace the autocratic form of government with a constitutional monarchy.

One forceful soldier-activist was Colonel Paul Pestel, a member of the nobility. More extreme than some of the other reformers, he wanted to establish a republic and was prepared to use any and all means to achieve it. His plan was to execute the Tsar and his imperial family and set up a temporary military dictatorship in order to institute sweeping reforms. These would include the emancipation of the serfs, elimination of class distinctions and the nationalization of all private landholdings. His ultimate goal was a republic in which administrative power would be held by a small, centralized hierarchy.

Pestel's opportunity came in 1825, following the death of Tsar Alexander I. For a time there was considerable confusion as to who would succeed him to the throne. Alexander's only son, the direct heir, had died some years before. The next in line would have been Alexander's brother Constantine. But he had secretly renounced the throne in favor of his younger brother Nicholas in order to marry a commoner. Now that Alexander was dead, Nicholas was reluctant to take the initiative in announcing his claim to the throne. Since the agreement had never been disclosed, he felt that the people would think he was trying to seize power from Constantine. In order to head off civil strife, he decided to do nothing until Constantine made his position known to the public.

Paul Pestel saw in the confusion and delay the chance he had been waiting for. He and his followers made hasty plans to seize the government. By the time the issue of succession was clarified and Nicholas was ready to ascend the throne, Pestel was prepared to strike. The time of the revolt was set to coincide with the ceremony at which Nicholas was to take his oath as Tsar!

Alerted by informers, the police and government troops moved in and made short work of the revolutionaries. The fighting, which was to become known as the Decembrist Uprising, was fierce and bloody. Pestel and many of his followers were arrested. Some were jailed or exiled to Siberia. Colonel Pestel and four other ringleaders were hanged—although capital punishment had been outlawed in Russia seventy-five years earlier.

While the Decembrists had lost their bid for power, their ideas did not die with their leaders. Pestel's philosophy of social revolution and violence foreshadowed things to come in Russia. Within two decades of his death a new radical ideology began to take shape. In some respects it bore a resemblance to Pestel's own concepts. The initial impetus came from secret revolutionary societies in France which subscribed to a doctrine known as Communism, from the Latin *communis*, meaning common or general. Communism was distinguished from Socialism, a more moderate philosophy that shunned violence, by its call for the complete overthrow of the existing social and political order.

In the late 1840's, a German workers' group in London began to call itself the Communist League. Seeking a detailed program that would conform to their revolutionary premise, they asked a German-born philosopher-journalist named Karl Marx to help. He agreed to prepare such a platform in collaboration with a colleague, a wealthy young fellow countryman, Friedrich Engels.

The document was published in February of 1848. Marx and Engels called it *The Communist Manifesto*. The slim, unimposing volume became the bible of revolution in every corner of the globe.

The bomb that killed Tsar Alexander II in March of 1881 was the result of a plot by a handful of terrorists. Yet in a real sense the explosion was an echo of the doctrine of violence as propounded by Paul Pestel and the philosophy of revolution as enunciated by Marx and Engels. . . .

The conspiracy to kill Tsar Alexander III in which Alexander Ulyanov was implicated was hatched in February of 1887. Although Alexander was a participant, he was not the ringleader. The key organizer was a pale, sickly young man named Pyotr Shevyrev. An intense and convincing speaker, Shevyrev persuaded his comrades that a successful assassination would be a real blow for freedom.

The feverish planning was carried out in a spirit of romantic excitement and secrecy. Alexander did not even breathe a word of it to his sister Anna. One of the plotters suggested that the deed would be more dramatic if carried out on March 13, the anniversary of the assassination of Tsar Alexander II. The rest agreed.

From the start, there was an amateurish, almost pitiful quality to the conspiracy. The would-be terrorists had no money, organization or training. Alexander sold for a hundred rubles a gold medal he had received for scholastic excellence. The group used some of this money to obtain two secondhand pistols and ammunition.

Because of his science background, Alexander was assigned to manufacture bombs. Since he knew nothing of bomb-making, he read up on explosives in the library. The result was a strange-looking device of his own design consisting of a metal container filled with homemade dynamite.

At last everything was ready. As the fateful day neared, the plotters were in a state of feverish excitement. Alexander had made three dynamite bombs. One was to be concealed in a hollowed-out medical dictionary and carried by one of three students—Alexander was not in the group—who were chosen as the "bomb-throwing squad." The other two would carry the remaining bombs and the two pistols in their coats. The extra bombs and the guns were to be used if the first bomb failed to kill the Tsar or if they were needed to help the terrorists make their escape.

It had been announced that Alexander III would make a ceremonial inspection of St. Petersburg on March 1. On these tours his carriage usually carried him along the Nevsky Prospect, a broad boulevard that cut through the heart of the Russian capital. So on March 11, the bomb-throwers paid an advance visit to the Nevsky Prospect to choose the best site for the assassination.

The three were already under the scrutiny of police detectives.

Official interest in the strange behavior of the students on the Nevsky Prospect had its origin in a letter intercepted by the police many weeks earlier. It had been sent by one of the three—a boy named Andreyushkin—to a student friend in Kharkov. It was a long, confused letter justifying the use of terrorism to achieve political ends. Although no specific mention was made of a bomb plot, the inflammatory contents ignited the interest of the secret police, who placed Andreyushkin under surveillance.

After shadowing the student and his two companions to the Nevsky Prospect the detectives were convinced they were up to some mischief. But they had no basis for making arrests.

On March 13, the day of the Tsar's inspection tour, the police again followed the three to the boulevard. This time Andreyushkin carried a suspiciously large book, and the other two appeared to be concealing objects in their pockets. The detectives stopped the students, identified themselves as police officers and examined the book. They were astonished to find that it was hollow and contained a bomb.

One of the students drew his pistol and fired point-blank at the police. The weapon failed to discharge. The detectives disarmed him and led all three off to the police station for a more complete search. As soon as they entered the station house, Osipanov hastily removed a cardboard box from his coat pocket and hurled it to the floor. The bomb did not explode.

Intensive questioning quickly loosened the tongues of the amateur assassins and they began to talk freely. They gave the police the names of their associates and the details of the plot. The police began to round up the other conspirators. They arrived at the lodginghouse where Alexander Ulyanov lived and found his sister Anna waiting for him. The detectives arrested her on suspicion and picked up her brother a short time later.

In all, seventy-four were taken into custody. They included not only the conspirators but many of their friends who had been ignorant of the plot. Most were released for lack of evidence. Alexander and Anna Ulyanov were among those arraigned and held.

Although Alexander readily admitted his guilt, those who knew him could scarcely believe it. They were at a loss to understand how a quiet, gentle young man could turn into a terrorist almost overnight. Some recalled his emotional reaction to his father's death less than a year before and speculated that his mind had snapped. Others felt that he had sought revenge against the Tsar for the shabby way Ilya had been treated by the Ministry of Education.

When Maria Alexandrovna Ulyanov arrived in St. Petersburg, her single goal was to help Alexander and Anna. She was not concerned with their guilt or innocence or why her son had taken part in the plot. Her purpose was to save her children, not judge them.

Some members of her father's family, the Blanks, occupied high posts in the government. Her first step was to approach them for help in obtaining the Tsar's permission to visit Alexander in the jail where he was being held for trial.

Alexander III granted the request. He wrote: "I think it would be advisable to allow her to see her son so that she can see for herself what kind of person this precious son of hers is."

When Maria Alexandrovna was taken to Alexander's cell, he broke down and wept. However, after wiping his eyes he was the same as always—calm and self-contained. He did not try to explain what had driven him to terrorism, nor did he indicate a sense of remorse. If anything, he appeared to be exalted, almost proud of what he had done. When his mother tried to discuss his approaching trial, he replied that he was completely indifferent to his fate.

The trial took place in St. Petersburg in early spring and commanded a great deal of public attention. Only fifteen of all those originally arrested were tried. The defendants included some, like Anna, whose link to the assassination plot was based not on evidence but on a close relationship to one of the key conspirators.

The defense attorneys pleaded that their clients were misguided young people who really did not understand what they were doing. Yet when the principal defendants were called upon to speak in their own behalf toward the end of the trial they made no attempt to hide their guilt. To the consternation of their lawyers, they made it clear that they were aware of the nature of their actions and were prepared to accept the consequences. At one point, Alexander whispered to one of the minor defendants, "If you need to, put all the blame upon me!"

The drama of the trial reached its peak when Alexander was called upon to address the court. He spoke of the discontent with the present social order, the inevitability of revolution and the justification for using terror. Terror, he declared, was the only method left to intellectuals, since all other methods had failed. It was the weapon by which men could fight for their right to think freely, without government approval. He paused, then told his judges: "There is no finer death than death for one's country's sake; such a death holds no terror for sincere and honest men. I had but one aim: to help the unfortunate Russian people."

Maria Alexandrovna—who had been given special permission to

attend her children's trial—was amazed at his eloquence. It was a side of her silent Alexander that she had never seen before. Even the government prosecutor was moved. He admitted to the court that he admired the youth's candor and idealism, even though he could not agree with his philosophy.

By refusing to ask for mercy, Alexander and four other principal conspirators sealed their fate. Instead of short prison terms, which their lawyers had been seeking, the five were sentenced to death by hanging. Several of the others were given long prison terms. And Anna, whose innocence had been clearly established, was freed but told to remain under police supervision.

Even the Tsar, in reviewing the record of the case, was impressed by the honesty of Alexander Ulyanov's courtroom statement. Alongside the transcript of the youth's remarks he scribbled, "This frankness is even touching." But he refused to commute the death sentence.

Maria Alexandrovna accepted her son's fate with an air of quiet despair. It was almost as if she had sensed all along that in spite of her desperate efforts to save him, he had willed his own destiny from the start. She stayed in St. Petersburg to be as near him as possible until the day of his execution.

On May 20, 1887, Alexander Ulyanov and his four youthful comrades were hanged in the courtyard of St. Petersburg's Schlüsselburg fortress. Even at the very end, he was calm and controlled, almost serene.

Maria Alexandrovna sent Vladimir a telegram informing him of his brother's death. Then she left the capital for the long, lonely journey home.

When she arrived in Simbirsk she did not ring or knock but entered the house on Moskovskaya Street through the back door. The younger children cried as they crowded around and clung to their mother. Although she had been away only three months, she appeared to have aged, for her hair, dark before, had gone quite gray.

Vladimir remained dry-eyed. He did his best not to show emotion, for he did not want to add to the turmoil and sorrow in the household. Now that Alexander was gone, he felt it was up to him to set an example that would help calm and reassure his mother, brothers and sisters.

Just as he had done after his father's death, Vladimir plunged into his studies with a burst of renewed energy. Since he would be graduating from gymnasium in a few weeks, he had applied for permission to sit for a school certificate examination which would enable him to enter a university. The request had been granted by Feodor Kerensky, director of the gymnasium. Vladimir spared no time or effort to prepare for the examination. He studied as though he were at the foot of his class instead of the top. It was almost as if he felt called upon to make the highest possible grades in order to prove himself and rescue the name of Ulyanov from disgrace.

Vladimir passed the examination with honors. He also received perfect class grades in Latin, Greek, Russian, German, Slavonic, Scripture, mathematics, history, physics and geography. Logic was the only course in which his mark was slightly less than perfect. For his academic achievements he was named to receive the school's gold medal for excellence. Kerensky received a reproof from his superiors for awarding the medal to the younger brother of a hanged terrorist. Nevertheless, the gymnasium director stubbornly insisted that Vladimir Ulyanov had earned the award and therefore was entitled to it. The Ministry of Education dropped the subject for fear of creating an embarrassing public issue.

Shortly after the end of the school year, Vladimir sent an application to the University of Kazan requesting admission to the school of law. Kerensky had felt his prize student would be better suited to the school of literature and letters than law. However, when the youth insisted on clinging to his original choice, Kerensky wrote a glowing recommendation to the rector of the faculty of law at Kazan. The application for admission was approved.

Late in August of 1887, Vladimir Ilyich Ulyanov boarded the Volga steamer at Simbirsk for the 120-mile trip north to Kazan. The deaths of his father and brother were still painfully fresh in his mind as the vessel plowed slowly upstream.

4.

Birth of a Revolutionary

A FEW WEEKS LATER, the rest of the Ulyanov family followed Vladimir to Kazan. His mother sold the house and furniture, packed their personal belongings and left Simbirsk forever.

Maria Alexandrovna felt there was no longer any reason to remain in the town. Simbirsk was linked inextricably in her mind with the bitter memory of two recent tragedies. Kazan, on the other hand, was a thriving city of respectable size where she and the children could maintain their privacy and make a fresh start. Furthermore, it was important to her to keep the family together, for in the wake of calamity they had learned to cling to each other for mutual support and comfort.

The Ulyanovs rented an apartment on the Pervaya Gora, a fashionable street near the University of Kazan. The convenient location enabled Vladimir to live at home and walk to his classes.

Only Anna could not be with them. Even though she had been acquitted, the court had insisted that she remain under surveillance. To enable the police to keep an eye on her, the authorities barred her from living within city limits during the probationary period— a common practice in tsarist Russia.

Anna had chosen to stay at Kukushkino, the rural estate owned by the Blank family. There she would be near relatives and close enough to Kazan to receive regular visits from her mother, brothers and sisters.

For Vladimir, the University of Kazan opened up a world of new experiences. Freed from the rigid regulations of the gymnasium, he began to feel grown up at last. Here there was no daily inspection of notebooks and homework assignments, nor did the professors seem much concerned with student attendance.

Nevertheless, Vladimir was a model university student. He went to his classes regularly, spent much time in the library and prepared his reports with meticulous care. In truth, he was following a deliberately cautious path because he had promised his mother that he would avoid doing anything that might draw attention to himself. They both realized that as the brother of an executed terrorist, he would be under the rigid scrutiny of the university officials, possibly even the police. Therefore, he must do nothing that would jeopardize his education or his future.

The radical student groups soon learned of his presence and competed with each other to entice him into their activities. Among these organizations the late Alexander Ulyanov was a revered figure. To recruit the younger brother of a martyred hero into their ranks would be a coup. But Vladimir rejected their persistent invitations to attend meetings and refused to have anything to do with them.

The law clearly offered Vladimir a promising career. But it appeared that there were unconscious motivations for his choice as well, stemming from his brother's execution. He had followed the course of the trial carefully and had been in turn horrified and fascinated by it. He had been taught by his father to respect the law. It had been an article of faith with the older Ulyanov—one which young Vladimir had accepted without question. In spite of Alexander's tragic fate, he continued to believe in the ultimate power of the law to render justice and correct inequities. Shortly after Alexander's death, Vladimir had told his mother and sister Anna that the political path chosen by his brother had been wrong. He made it clear that he himself had no interest in revolution, nor could he—with all due respect to Alexander's sainted memory—even conceive of becoming a revolutionary. No, if Russia were to be changed for the better, he declared, it would have to be done legally, not by violence. And the key to such change lay in the hands of the lawyers, not in the bombs of the terrorists.

That autumn, the University of Kazan seethed with student unrest. The Ministry of Education, badly shaken by the student plot to assassinate the Tsar, assumed that all universities were hotbeds of terrorism. Accordingly, directives were issued to the university administrators to clamp down. Any professor who was even suspected of liberal tendencies was dismissed summarily. An earlier ban on student political groups was extended to include nonpolitical fraternal organizations as well.

Student reaction was characteristically swift and strong. Meetings were held at universities across Russia. On December 4 an assembly was called at the University of Kazan to protest the actions of the Ministry of Education. A large part of the student body turned out. Vladimir felt that as a student he had to show his support by attending even though he had no active part in the proceedings. Indeed, remembering his pledge to his mother, he hoped to remain as inconspicuous as possible.

At the assembly, a respectful, carefully worded petition was approved overwhelmingly. It was to be presented to the local school inspector for transmittal to the Ministry of Education.

As the audience left the meeting hall they were startled to find police inspectors at the doors. Each student was made to surrender his university registration card.

That night the police called at the Ulyanov apartment and announced that Vladimir was under arrest! Maria Alexandrovna's pleas and protests were turned brusquely aside. Vladimir was taken down to the police station and booked, along with thirty-nine other students.

Although no trial was held, the students were kept in jail for several days before being released. A report on Vladimir, transmitted by the police to the rector of the School of Law, read in part: "In view of the exceptional circumstances surrounding the Ulyanov family, the behavior of Ulyanov at the meeting gave the inspectors ground for believing that he was quite capable of various kinds of legal and criminal demonstrations."

Vladimir was formally expelled from the University of Kazan. He was also ordered to leave the city of Kazan and directed to remain under police surveillance.

Distraught almost to despair, his mother appealed to the authorities for permission to have her son remain at the Kukushkino estate, thirty miles from Kazan, with his sister Anna. This request was granted.

At first, Vladimir was overcome by bitterness. At seventeen, his promising university career had ended in disgrace after only three months. The attitude of the police in arresting him without bringing charges convinced him that innocence or guilt had had nothing to do with it. He had been completely innocent, had not uttered a single word at the assembly, yet that had not stopped the police from taking him into custody or the university from expelling him. It was clear now that the real charges against him were (1) that his name was Ulyanov and (2) that he was the brother of an executed terrorist. He was further convinced that the authorities had indeed kept an eye on him from the time he had entered the university. Thus they had judged him guilty from the start, and his presence at the assembly merely provided them with confirmation of their verdict-in-advance.

Nevertheless, Vladimir soon discovered that it was difficult for him to sustain his anger indefinitely. After a few days at Kukushkino, his bitterness subsided and he began to accept his expulsion more philosophically. He decided that there were worse fates than being exiled to the family estate. At Kukushkino loneliness was no problem. In addition to his sister Anna there were several aunts and cousins; and Anna's fiancé, a pleasant, intelligent insurance agent named Mark Elisarov, visited regularly. Elisarov turned out to be an excellent chess opponent for Vladimir.

Maria Alexandrovna settled her affairs in Kazan and moved to Kukushkino, bringing the other Ulyanov children. Vladimir's spirits took a turn for the better when his mother told him that there was a possibility of appealing for reinstatement at the university. Having consulted with relatives in government, she had been advised that the request might be approved, provided they waited a few months for the climate at the Ministry of Education to change.

The thousand-acre Blank estate was a marvelously rustic place with broad fields, great stands of tall trees and a swift-running stream alive with fish. The main structure was a sturdy old manor house that had a lived-in coziness reminiscent of the former Ulyanov home in Simbirsk. That winter, the snow blanketed the estate constantly. It trimmed the branches of the trees with jeweled decorations in an endless variety of shapes. And since the roads were almost impassable, there were few visitors except for Elisarov and the local police inspector who came by to see that Vladimir and Anna were behaving themselves.

Since Vladimir enjoyed cold weather, he loved to don his heavy overcoat and fur cap and go hunting or hiking. Elisarov joined him occasionally, but most of the time he went off by himself. Although he carried a rifle under his arm, he was not a hunter at heart. Not once during those months did he return with a single piece of game. In addition to being a poor marksman he could not bring himself to shoot at an animal. Recognizing this trait of his, he readily joined in the family laughter when he returned from a "hunting trip" empty-handed.

Vladimir's main occupation during his winter of exile was reading. He read everything he could find. Grandfather Blank had maintained a voluminous library of books and periodicals which he devoured. Arrangements were also made to have books sent by post from the university library in Kazan. And Elisarov and the few others who came to visit invariably brought him additional volumes. Newspapers from as far away as St. Petersburg and Moscow came with every mail delivery.

Most of his reading still consisted of novels or works of nonfiction dealing with language and literature. But some of the volumes sent from the University of Kazan were textbooks to help him keep up with his law studies.

Controversial books and pamphlets about politics or economics never entered the house. Not only did Vladimir still lack interest in these subjects, but he feared the police would find them. One unfortunate incident might eliminate any possibility of his readmission to the university.

Guarding constantly against any act—no matter how innocent—that might place him or the family in further jeopardy was a nerve-wracking necessity. Once he wrote a long, emotional account of his expulsion to a friend. He protested his innocence and denounced the university officials and the Ministry of Education for their actions. When Anna learned of it, she was horrified and warned that he must not send it. Didn't he realize that his mail was probably being censored? She pointed out that the letter would place his friend as well as himself in grave danger. At first Vladimir pooh-poohed her fears and insisted that it be sent. But when Anna reminded him that just such a letter, written by a St. Petersburg student to a friend, had led to his brother's arrest and execution, he realized she was right. The letter was destroyed.

With the coming of the spring thaw, the white fields and trees were magically transformed into a panorama of lush green. Vladimir continued his long walks in the countryside. Usually he carried a novel or book of poetry which he read while sprawled out in the shade of a great-branched linden tree. He also erected outdoor crossbars and exercised constantly to build his muscles.

In early May of 1888, some five months after his expulsion, Vladimir formally applied for readmission to the university. The local police inspector had notified him that his term of surveillance was ended. Consequently, it was agreed that the time was favorable for an appeal.

For several weeks, the Ulyanovs waited hopefully for the application to be acted upon by the Ministry of Education. Each day that passed without a reply encouraged them to feel that Vladimir's chances were improving.

Finally the anxiously awaited answer came in the post. The letter was written in formal, almost brusque language. It informed Vladimir that his request for readmission could not be considered. The news cast a pall of gloom over Kukushkino. Maria Alexandrovna was almost heartbroken.

Nevertheless, throughout the summer she stubbornly continued to write letters to friends and relatives seeking help in having the decision rescinded. To her, education was so important that she refused to entertain the notion that it might be permanently denied her son. Additional inquiries were made at high governmental levels. The reports that came back were always the same. The case was a closed book as far as the Ministry of Education was concerned. The administrators were convinced that to readmit Vladimir Ulyanov, brother of an executed terrorist, to any Russian university was too risky under any circumstances.

By September, the Ulyanovs were desperate enough to grasp at any straw. Perhaps Vladimir could study at a foreign university? Since permission of the Minister of the Interior was required to leave the country, a letter was carefully composed seeking such approval. The request pointed out that since he no longer could study in a Russian institution, it was necessary for him to attend a foreign university "to support his family and acquire a higher education."

This plea, too, was rejected. But one small boon was granted: Vladimir was given permission to return to Kazan to live. As a result, the family made plans to return to the city at once. An apartment was rented on the same street as before—the Pervaya Gora near the university—for Maria Alexandrovna refused to abandon hope that her son might be given another chance. Anna, whose term of police supervision still had some months to go, was forced to remain at Kukushkino. There, she was kept busy making plans for her forthcoming marriage to Mark Elisarov.

The new apartment in Kazan was spacious. It had an extra kitchen which Vladimir took over as a study. He spent most of his days here, poring through books which lined the pantry shelves and every other available inch of space. When he did leave the kitchen-study it was usually to run an errand for his mother or visit the university library at which he still had borrowing privileges.

One day a friend loaned him a book that set off a sharp pang of painful memory. It was Karl Marx's *Capital,* the work that had so engrossed Alexander. In contrast to his earlier lack of interest, Vladimir was now drawn to it like a magnet. Out of sheer curiosity, he leafed through the pages wondering what it was about Marx's writing that had influenced his brother's life so profoundly. He became so absorbed in the book that he could not put it down. He spent many days and much of his nights analyzing *Capital,* and in the end he was able to repeat some of the passages by heart.

What Vladimir found most compelling was the clarity and precision with which Marx defined the structure of society. In the pages of *Capital,* there were no obscure philosophical questions, no polite evasions in discussing the problems plaguing mankind. Marx provided a clear, simple formula for interpreting history and curing all social and economic ills. He called his doctrine "scientific socialism."

The concept of socialism was not new. For decades numerous reformers had opposed the oppression of the masses and advocated that peasants and workers be given a greater share in the economy. They foresaw a time when the propertied classes would realize that their own self-interest lay in alleviating poverty and suffering by curbing exploitation of the poor. Some of these advocates were known as "utopian socialists." They sought to effect change through the use of education, political influence and other peaceful methods of persuasion. Violence was opposed.

The "scientific socialism" of Marx contemptuously dismissed the theories of these peaceful socialists as unrealistic and useless. Socialism, Marx claimed, could not be brought about peacefully. It could only be effected by overthrowing the entire system under which society was governed.

According to Marxist doctrine, the advent of a socialistic revolution was not an isolated happening. It was an inevitable step in the forward march of history. History itself, he argued, was an immutable unfolding of events which were not accidental but the result of rigid natural laws. And these laws were as universally applicable as the laws of chemistry or physics.

Before Marx, many philosophers and historians had tried to devise a simple and direct formula that would enable them to interpret —and predict—the course of history. Some asserted that the type of leadership was the most important factor in society's development. They claimed that great leaders brought progress and poor leaders were responsible for mankind's misfortunes. Others felt that history could be charted according to changes in religious doctrine.

Marx, however, argued for an economic interpretation of history. He declared that every event could be understood in the light of economic relationships. How goods are produced, traded and distributed was the real key to understanding human social development.

According to this theory, control of any society stemmed from ownership of the means of production. In an agricultural society, those who owned the land became the ruling class. In an industrial era, the owners of the factories and machines were the real rulers who controlled all phases of political, economic and social life.

Marx also was convinced that those who ruled any society did so exclusively in their own interest and would not willingly give up power. Indeed, they would use every means at their disposal to protect their interests. Therefore, he reasoned, the masses must seize control from the ruling classes through "class struggle." And since all political and other institutions in a given society—including the government itself—were under the domination of the ruling classes, they must be destroyed through revolution. Once the struggle was resolved in the interest of the masses, the revolution would end. Ultimately, Marx predicted, governments would disappear—for they were merely the tools by which rulers kept people in chains and would no longer be necessary once the masses seized control.

According to *Capital*, class struggle was a recurring sequence in historical development. It was also inevitable, for the economic laws determining history are rigid and allow for no exceptions. The first step in the Marxist historical pattern was conflict between aristocrats and commoners, such as the patricians and plebeians of the early days of ancient Rome. The second sequence was struggle between freemen and slaves, as in later ancient Rome. The next step was seen by Marx as class conflict between feudal lords and peasants, as exemplified in the Middle Ages. The fourth and final step was the clash between the bourgeoisie, or middle class, and the proletariat, those who worked for wages in a modern, industrial society.

In *Capital* industrial progress was not condemned; it was welcomed, since under Marxist theory it hastened the final victory of the masses over the ruling classes. Inevitably, in the historic progression, the bourgeois, or capitalist, class was doomed to dig its own grave. Since improved machines and factories meant less demand for human labor, lower wages and increased joblessness would result. The miserable lot of the worker would be intensified until he could endure it no longer and would rise against his capitalist masters. The task of dedicated Communists, Marx declared, was to help the proletariat understand its predicament, thus speeding the overthrow of capitalism.

Marx was vague about when this revolution would occur. He stressed that it would happen only after the completion of the capitalist cycle—no sooner and no later. Like the earlier steps in the sequence, there could be no deviation in the preset pattern of history.

Vladimir was understandably excited by his discovery of Marx's writings. It opened up new horizons which he had never dreamed of before. The certainty and simplicity of Communist doctrine had an appeal for an eighteen-year-old in search of a cause. He was so elated by Marxist philosophy that he could not resist sharing it with whoever was around at the moment. Hardly a day passed that he did not come racing out of his study to read a particular sentence or paragraph to his mother, explaining with excited gestures what he felt it meant.

However, Maria Alexandrovna did not view his sudden interest in Marx complacently. Her biggest fear was that he would follow in Alexander's steps and become a revolutionary. With her oldest son in the grave, she was horrified to think that Vladimir, too, might someday end up in prison, or worse. Yet she understood her children too well to think that she could talk him out of his preoccupation with Marx. Instead, she searched for a way to divert his interest from politics. And in the spring of 1889, she was convinced she had found it.

Since all doors to higher education and a profession had been closed to Vladimir, his mother decided to buy a large farm. As a landowner and gentleman farmer, he would have an occupation and guaranteed income. She recalled that her own father had retired from medicine soon after buying the Kukushkino estate and had managed to acquire enough wealth from the land to leave a handsome legacy to his children. Why could not someone with Vladimir's brains do equally well? Besides, a large estate would enable the entire family, including Anna and her husband-to-be, to live close together. This was Maria Alexandrovna's treasured dream: a secure and peaceful future in which they could begin to forget the tragic events of recent years.

Through her future son-in-law, she heard of an estate for sale near Samara, a city on the Volga 150 miles south of Kazan. Mark Elisarov had been brought up in a village near Samara and knew the region well. The farm in question was 225 acres, with a mill, stables and large rambling manor house. The estate was worked by eighty-four *muzhiks*, or peasants, who lived nearby with their families. With Elisarov's help Maria Alexandrovna was able to purchase it for 7,500 rubles, the amount she had received from the sale of her house in Simbirsk. It was a bargain price.

The family moved to Samara early in May of 1889, soon after Anna was released from police supervision and permitted to leave Kukushkino.

It had been agreed that Vladimir and Elisarov would be jointly in charge of operating the estate. Although Vladimir was less than enthusiastic at the notion of becoming a landlord and "exploiter of peasants," he threw himself into the work with characteristic determination. Nevertheless, it was clear after a few months that he lacked the instinct for farming. So did Elisarov, the good-natured, outgoing insurance agent who was a city man in his soul. Ultimately, Maria Alexandrovna had to put the management of the farm in the hands of an experienced land agent who agreed to work it for a fee.

Left to his own interests once more, Vladimir returned to his books. He read every morning and most afternoons, concentrating on the works of Marx and other writers on social and economic issues. He also tutored his brothers and sisters, played chess with Elisarov or his younger brother, Dmitry, and took long strolls in the countryside.

Although Vladimir's failure as a lord of the manor disappointed his mother, she was not deeply distressed. Nor did his return to Marxist reading worry her as much as it had in Kazan. Here, on the estate, they were together as a family, isolated from the rest of the world. Thus, there was little chance that Vladimir would get into trouble. She felt a sense of peace and contentment that she had not enjoyed since before the death of her husband. Often on a quiet summer evening, the family would gather on the porch after supper and a pail of cool milk would be fetched from the cellar. Then, amid the soft silence of the darkening steppes, they would talk or sing folk songs until it was time to go to bed. On such perfect evenings, Maria Alexandrovna Ulyanov was so overcome with emotion that she was moved to wish aloud that things would always remain this way.

5.

Appointment in St. Petersburg

MARIA ALEXANDROVNA originally planned to have the estate serve as the family's all-season home. But with the employment of a professional manager, it was no longer necessary for the Ulyanovs to remain there on a year-round basis. Besides, the isolation of country life—particularly during the long, cruel winters—was hard on the children. Accustomed to town living and superior city schools, they clamored for a chance to spend at least part of the year in Samara itself.

Maria Alexandrovna finally gave in. She rented a large apartment in town as their official residence. The estate was to serve as a retreat for summer vacations and holidays.

In Samara, Vladimir made a number of new friends. Many were introduced to him through his brother-in-law, Mark Elisarov. He was especially fond of Andrey Khardin, a lawyer and noted chess player. In addition to playing chess, Vladimir and the attorney had long, serious discussions about Russian politics. Khardin was a moderate liberal who disputed many facets of Marxist doctrine. To the youth, who was preoccupied with Marx, it was a challenge that could not be ignored. He defended the German philosopher's ideas vigorously, even heatedly.

Elisarov's friends ranged politically from liberals like Khardin to radicals who were fully committed to the concept of revolution. A number of the latter met clandestinely as a study group. Vladimir got to know these militants. In spite of his mother's grave fears, he soon became a member of the circle and attended its meetings. While the police were aware of the existence of the group, they did not feel it represented a grave enough threat to require close surveillance.

In the meantime the question of Vladimir's career continued to plague him and his mother. At twenty, he was already troubled by a sense of failure. With no training for a profession the future seemed bleak.

Then his discussions with Andrey Khardin opened up a new horizon. Learning of his interest in law, the attorney advised him that in special cases students were permitted to sit for the law examinations without actually attending a university. Vladimir was jubilant. But Khardin warned him that even if permission were granted, it was not easy to master a four-year curriculum through self-study. It meant months of concentrated reading in subjects that were difficult enough to comprehend even in a classroom with knowledgeable professors. Vladimir, however, had no reservations about going ahead. In truth, he had no alternative.

In the fall of 1890, he posted a request to the Ministry of Education for permission to sit for the law examination. It was promptly refused. Disappointed again but still not prepared to give up, Maria Alexandrovna took matters into her own hands. She dispatched a personal letter to the Minister, appealing as a "widow and a mother." She reminded him of her late husband's position as a nobleman stemming from his services to Russia. Pointing out her pain at seeing her son waste "the best years of his life without being able to make use of them," she pleaded that the government relent in its position.

This time the sensibilities of the Minister were stirred. Maria Alexandrovna received a reply stating that permission had been granted for Vladimir to sit for the law examination!

The Ulyanovs were almost unprepared for the good news. Years of tragedy and discouragement had taught them to accept disappointment as a way of life. Now it was difficult for them to react with wholehearted enthusiasm to the favorable turn of events. It was almost as though they feared that by showing unrestrained joy they would be tempting misfortune to strike again.

Vladimir threw himself completely into his law studies. He was determined to pass the examination with highest honors, as if to prove that his expulsion from the university had not really mattered after all. Every other activity and interest were forgotten. Even Karl Marx was thrust aside for the time being.

In May of 1891, as he was about to take the preliminary law examination, a new sorrow beset the Ulyanov family.

Vladimir had traveled to St. Petersburg for the examination. While in the capital he visited his sister Olga, two years his junior, who had gone there earlier. At nineteen, Olga was a charming young lady who had been a brilliant student at the gymnasium. Although she would have preferred to become a physician, women were not permitted to study medicine in Russia. Accordingly, she had settled on teaching and was in St. Petersburg to take courses at a teachers' institute.

Vladimir noticed that Olga seemed unusually tired. When she became feverish, he grew worried and took her to a hospital. The diagnosis was typhoid fever and she was immediately put to bed. Vladimir sent his mother a telegram informing her of Olga's illness. Maria Alexandrovna wired that she was coming to St. Petersburg at once. In the meantime Olga's condition was complicated by a throat infection, and she grew worse.

Mrs. Ulyanov arrived in the capital in time to see her daughter die. Vladimir noted sorrowfully that the date was May 20, the fourth anniversary of his brother's execution.

Somehow, in spite of this latest tragedy, he managed to sit through the preliminary examination and pass it with high marks. Several months later he returned to St. Petersburg for the final law examination. He felt he had done well, but when the grades were published and he learned that he was *first* among the 124 candidates, even he was surprised. Completely self-taught, he had mastered in less than a year a course that normally took four years! In November of 1891, he became a full-fledged advocate, licensed to practice before a court of law. However, what should have been a time of rejoicing for the Ulyanov family was tempered by grief over the death of lovely Olga.

Vladimir took a job as a junior attorney with Andrey Khardin. But he soon realized that practicing law was not the exciting battle for justice that he had once imagined. Most of the work consisted of preparing routine briefs and contracts. Occasionally he defended peasants charged with petty crimes, but he found law dreary, uninspiring work.

His most interesting case was one that he handled without fee, since he was his own client. One day he and Elisarov set out to visit Mark's brother in the village of Bestuzhevka, on the east bank of the Volga. Most people crossed the river on a steam ferry owned by a merchant named Arefyev. But impatient Vladimir suggested that rather than wait for the ferry to fill with passengers, they hire a nearby boatman to row them across.

Arefyev saw them talking to the boatman and guessed what was up. He warned that since he was paying money to the government for the privilege of ferrying passengers, he could not permit a private boatman to take them over. Vladimir replied with some heat that no one had a right to obstruct him as he went about his lawful affairs. Then he and Elisarov climbed into the boat and instructed the boatman to begin rowing. Furious, Arefyev directed the ferry captain to pursue the small boat. Halfway across, the larger craft caught up to the rowboat, threw down grappling hooks and forced it to return to the west bank.

Vladimir hailed the merchant into court on a charge of interfering with his lawful passage. Arefyev employed various delaying tactics in the hope of discouraging the young lawyer and preventing the case from coming to trial. But Vladimir kept after his adversary with the tenacity of a bulldog, even though it meant traveling more than seventy miles for each court hearing. The case dragged on for more than a year. In the end, Arefyev was sentenced to one month's imprisonment. For the young lawyer, the satisfaction of achieving a victory of basic principle far outweighed the time and effort he had devoted to the case.

Like his father, Vladimir began to lose his hair while still in his early twenties. It made him look older. Nevertheless, to make himself appear even more mature and inspire confidence in his few clients he grew a small reddish mustache and beard which he kept carefully trimmed.

Unfortunately, the touch of added dignity failed to attract new clients. Samara, like most of the Volga region, was suffering from a serious economic depression which affected all trades and professions.

The depression had been brought on by a devastating failure of the grain crops in 1891-92. Since starvation was widespread in the farming areas, the plight of the peasants was the main subject of conversation everywhere.

Vladimir saw the depression purely in Marxist terms and did not hesitate to point out that it was caused not by fate but by the failure of the government and private capitalism. He became more immersed than ever in revolutionary theory and met regularly with the small group of Samara radicals. At these gatherings, issues were hotly debated and the possible course of future events analyzed.

Increasingly, within this circle, Vladimir found himself defending unpopular views. One of the thorniest issues centered around the proper role of radicals during the famine. Relief committees had been organized throughout Russia to collect funds and provide emergency food rations for starving peasants. Many Russian liberals such as Leo Tolstoy, Vladimir's favorite author, threw themselves wholeheartedly into the relief effort in spite of their opposition to the Tsar's policies. In Samara, anyone who could spare a few rubles contributed to the emergency drive, including most radicals in Vladimir's circle. In spite of their revolutionary fervor, they felt that saving people from starvation was a humanitarian matter that should be divorced from politics. Not Vladimir. Taking Marxist dogma literally, he interpreted every Russian misfortune as a blessing, since it would help speed the inevitable revolution.

The difference of opinion within the radical movement developed into a bitter quarrel. The following year the grain grew in abundance and ended the famine; but the split between extremists like Vladimir and the moderates continued. It marked a growing cleavage that was to characterize Russian radicalism for decades to come.

The dispute also represented a critical turning point for Vladimir personally. By emerging as the spokesman for the small group of extreme Marxists, he had tasted the heady wine of leadership and found it to his liking. Now he realized that in political activity he had found his true role at last. In a few short years he had swung sharply from liberalism to Marxist radicalism. And he knew it was only a matter of time before conviction would lead him from intellectualizing about Marxism to revolutionary activism. For perhaps the first time, he began to understand the motives that had driven his brother Alexander to the acts of terrorism that had cost him his life.

While Vladimir knew that he would have to continue to work to support himself, the practice of law was now of secondary importance. His all-consuming interest was the politics of revolution. Marxism so dominated his thinking and reading that he had time for little else. His mother was dismayed to the point of despair. The political direction he had taken frightened her; yet she was powerless to do anything about it. At twenty-two he was wholly responsible for his own actions and no longer within the pale of her influence in matters of personal conviction.

Vladimir's accelerated drift toward the life of a revolutionary was accompanied by growing dissatisfaction with Samara. He found the city dull and boring, even suffocating. To pass the rest of his life there was inconceivable. In particular, it was so removed from the real scene of political activity that he might just as well be on the other side of the earth.

For months he dreamed of resettling in St. Petersburg, but his mother pleaded with him not to go. She needed him in Samara, and so did his younger brother and sister. So for a time Vladimir remained. But eventually he concluded that he must make his move or remain in Samara forever. Therefore, early in 1893, he announced that he planned to leave for St. Petersburg. Once more, Maria Alexandrovna did her best to dissuade him. This time he would not allow himself to be swayed. His mother knew then that she must learn to accept his decision as she had accepted so many other defeats and disappointments in recent years.

Vladimir arrived in St. Petersburg wearing his father's handsome old frock coat and top hat. He carried a battered piece of luggage and an armful of books. A lodginghouse recommended by a friend provided him with room and board for fifteen rubles a month.

Through other acquaintances, he obtained a job with a lawyer named M. F. Volkenstein. His duties were similar to those in Khardin's office in Samara. The salary was low but he was not concerned because his mother had promised to send a regular sum out of the income from the estate.

Since St. Petersburg was supposed to be the hub of revolutionary activity, Vladimir was anxious to make contact with the important leaders of the Marxist movement. It proved to be more complicated then he had thought. Following the famine, the Russian economy had recovered rapidly. Industry was growing, employment was booming and income was at a high level. Hundreds of thousands of peasants poured into the cities to take factory jobs. In such a time of record prosperity, revolution was hardly a popular cause. Besides, police spies were reputed to be everywhere and only the hardiest activists risked illegal political activity.

For months, Vladimir led a lonely, hermitlike existence, unable to make contact. He went to the law office daily and spent the long evenings reading every political book and tract he could find.

In the meantime, his mother wrote that she had decided to move the family to Moscow. Since the younger children, Maria and Dmitry, were approaching university age, she preferred Moscow University to the university in Kazan from which Vladimir had been expelled. In addition, Moscow was only four hundred miles from St. Petersburg, close enough for regular visits.

During the Christmas holidays of 1893, Vladimir took a train to Moscow to be with his family. One evening, he learned of a secret student meeting designed to bring together various revolutionary groups for an evening of debate. Through a Moscow girl he had once met in Samara, he obtained a ticket. The meeting took place in a small student apartment on a street near Moscow University. It was packed. One of the honored guests was a middle-aged physician named Vasily Vorontsov, who was well known as a veteran revolutionary. An authoritative writer and speaker, he proceeded to reject the Marxist thesis that the development of industrial capitalism was a necessary precondition for revolution. Vorontsov argued feelingly that the Russian masses could not afford to wait for capitalism to mature fully before striking it down. Capitalism, he warned, must be overthrown before it could take hold and dominate Russian society.

Vladimir was incensed. To a budding young radical whose god was Karl Marx, the words of the old revolutionary seemed blasphemous. Arising, he launched into a well-reasoned attack on Vorontsov's call to battle. Citing Marx from memory, he argued that a revolution launched before conditions were favorable was doomed to fail. The industrial working masses were the soldiers of revolution, he asserted. Without capitalism there could be no such army.

Vorontsov listened to the argument of the youthful upstart with visible anger. Although the audience was astonished at the boldness of the young visitor from St. Petersburg, it greeted his words with rapt attention. Vorontsov tried to rebut Vladimir, but proved to be no match for the younger man as a debater. In the end, he complained defensively that Vladimir had offered no proof for his statements and held no credentials as an authority. Boasting of the books he himself had written, Vorontsov demanded of his opponent: "What published works have come from your pen?"

The audience did not respond favorably to this line of attack. It was clear that the veteran radical was falling back on the well-known debater's trick of disparaging an opponent's qualifications when he could not destroy his arguments.

Word of Vladimir's victory over the renowned Vorontsov spread like wildfire through radical circles. By the time he returned to St. Petersburg, he was something of a hero. No longer was it necessary to search out fellow Marxists; now they came looking for him—to invite him to gatherings and participate in debates.

At one party, he met a small, delicate-looking girl dressed in plain black with her hair brushed straight back. Vladimir was immediately taken with her. Her name was Nadezhda Konstantinovna Krupskaya, and she was the daughter of a deceased army officer. Although a member of the Russian nobility, her father had been a liberal thinker. As military governor of a district in Russian-occupied Poland he had introduced many reforms, including the building of a hospital and school and the outlawing of anti-Jewish activity. These enlightened policies brought him popularity with the Poles but vilification by his superiors, who felt he was sabotaging the harsh program of Russification decreed by the Tsar.

Nadezhda's father was forced to leave the army and died when she was in her early teens, leaving his family deeply in debt. The young girl helped support the family by giving lessons. She also attended evening classes at the gymnasium. Repelled by oppression as her father had been, she eventually joined a Marxist study group in the hope of discovering answers to social problems that perplexed her. In addition, she gave time as a volunteer to a Committee on Literacy which was established by a small group of philanthropists to provide free reading instruction to illiterate workers.

Vladimir and Nadezhda began to see a great deal of each other. Through her, he became familiar with the work of the Committee on Literarcy. He saw in the organization a superb "cover" for recruiting workers to Marxism. They attended meetings and distributed illegal literature together. Their common political interest soon grew into romance.

From Nadezhda, Vladimir learned a great deal about the attitudes and prejudices of the common man—the proletariat. Because of his own protected middle-class background, his knowledge of the masses had come mainly from books and other indirect sources. But Nadezhda had personally suffered from poverty and had seen oppression with her own eyes. She could talk about it authoritatively. Vladimir, in turn, tried to explain to her the intellectual basis of Karl Marx's philosophy. However, inasmuch as Nadezhda's radicalism stemmed from an idealistic desire to relieve the oppressed, she never seemed able to master the more sophisticated facets of Communist dogma.

As he became more deeply involved with revolutionary groups, Vladimir's actions took on an increasingly conspiratorial tone. He soon mastered the techniques of secrecy and deception needed to keep a step ahead of the police. He learned to use roundabout routes and often changed from one droshky—a horse-drawn public carriage —to another to throw off agents who might be following. He also read up on the use of codes and secret inks. Frequently he resorted to disguises and false names to outwit spies who might be planted at political meetings.

For the moment, the Marxists considered their main function to be the spreading of their gospel among the working class. Accordingly, Vladimir spent most of his evenings secretly establishing "cells" of workers, usually six to a cell. Most of the workers were solicited through the Committee on Literacy. Using pseudonyms—he frequently called himself "Nikolay Petrovich"—he would talk with them about their problems, inquire about labor conditions and encourage them to hold future meetings.

It was not easy to convince the workers that the current prosperity would give way to hard times again, according to the inevitable Marxist timetable. Nevertheless, Vladimir was extremely effective as a propagandist. He employed simple logic spiced with broad generalizations and ringing slogans. There was about him an air of authority at all times. As a result, he quickly became one of the most successful and popular organizers in the radical movement.

The insights he gained from the workers on industrial conditions proved useful, too. They added to what he learned from Nadezhda and in turn enabled him to develop even more effective techniques to appeal to the self-interest of the workers.

Before settling in St. Petersburg, Vladimir had done almost no writing on political issues. Once, in Samara, he had prepared a lengthy review of a book dealing with agrarian problems. It was rejected by a magazine. But now he realized that to achieve his goal of becoming a revolutionary leader, he would have to circulate his ideas more widely. Therefore, he began writing a series of pamphlets giving his interpretation of Marxist doctrine.

Like his speeches, they were precise, simply worded and rhetorical. He employed anger, sarcasm and ridicule to put across an idea or demolish an opponent. When quoting Marx, he did not hesitate to cite isolated passages out of context to prove his point. Nor did he hesitate to justify the use of violence and terrorism as sometimes necessary to advance the interests of the proletariat. To Vladimir, who had accepted the Marxist notion that the end rather than the means is what is important, any device that hastened the revolution was justified.

At first, Nadezhda found it hard to accept this cynical doctrine. It seemed to violate the very spirit of idealism that had impelled her toward radical politics in the first place. But her love for the young revolutionary overcame her reservations. After all, he was the master of Marxist theory, and she was sadly naive in doctrinal matters. She decided that her duty was to show him loyalty and faith, even if it meant swallowing her doubts.

The spiritual leaders of Marxism in Russia were George Plekhanov and Paul Axelrod, two Russian exiles. Because of their revolutionary activities, both men had been forced to flee to Switzerland years before. In exile, Plekhanov, in particular, became a sort of legendary high priest of Russian radicalism to whom ambitious, promising young leaders looked for approval and guidance.

Plekhanov, like many other radical intellectuals, belonged to the nobility. But while still very young he had dedicated himself to the struggle against oppression of the masses. He had openly criticized the government and led public demonstrations. Eventually the threat of arrest had forced him to leave Russia. Now, in a villa in Switzerland, he wrote books on the nature of Marxist socialism which were read secretly and avidly by his followers in Russia.

By 1895, Vladimir's star had begun to shine brightly in St. Petersburg's revolutionary circles. It was bright enough to justify a trip to Switzerland to confer with Plekhanov and Axelrod. But in March a bout with pneumonia laid him low and brought his mother up from Moscow. She and Nadezhda took to each other at once, for in outlook and disposition they were very much alike. The two women nursed him back to partial health.

Although pale and still weak, Vladimir insisted on leaving for Switzerland at the end of April. He received some funds from the party's meager treasury and made up the rest out of his own pocket.

His poor health did not deter him from enjoying his first trip abroad immensely. The sights and sounds of other nations intrigued him, and he welcomed the chance to apply the knowledge of foreign languages he had acquired in school.

Vladimir met Plekhanov in Geneva, Switzerland. The Marxist leader was a tall, elegant man dressed in impeccable taste who dwarfed the short, red-bearded young lawyer. Although correct and courteous, Plekhanov seemed distant, almost aloof. Plekhanov had read some of Vladimir's pamphlets. He made it clear that he differed sharply with the violent tone of these writings. Plekhanov pointed out that more converts could be won to Marxism by intellectual persuasion than by insult and vituperation.

Somewhat disappointed, Vladimir journeyed from Geneva to Zurich, where he met Paul Axelrod. Axelrod was an excitable, shaggy-looking man, in contrast to Plekhanov's cool elegance. Yet his criticism of Vladimir's pamphlets was the same as Plekhanov's. He disagreed with their scornful, violent tone and argued that it was a mistake to revile liberals and other radicals such as Vorontsov who refused to accept Marxist doctrine as dogma. What was needed, Axelrod asserted, was a *common front* of all groups desiring the overthrow of the tsarist regime. Out of courtesy and respect to Axelrod, Vladimir conceded that this argument was a valid one and he would think about it. But secretly he continued to harbor distrust of all non-Marxists.

On other issues, he and Axelrod found themselves in harmony. The older man was impressed with Vladimir's report of his success in establishing secret cells of workers in St. Petersburg. They decided that the next step should be the transformation of these small groups from mere study circles into an active, unified political party.

They also agreed on the need to publish a political magazine. Although it would be printed abroad there would be important dispatches and articles smuggled out of Russia. In this way there would be constant communication, making for increased unity in the international revolutionary movement.

Instead of returning to Russia from Zurich, Vladimir decided to go on to France. He spent a month in Paris, walking the boulevards, studying the wares in the windows of fine shops in the Opera section and visiting museums and libraries. Duty impelled him to meet some of the leading French radicals to discuss political issues. But he found that summer is a poor time for concern with weighty matters when one is visiting Paris for the first time. Indeed, he was so fascinated with the city that he was quite content to put aside the grim tasks of revolution for the time being.

By mid-August, Vladimir was running short of money. He wrote to his mother and received a hundred rubles, which enabled him to proceed to Germany. Wandering through the streets of Berlin as he had done in Paris, he haunted the bookshops and absorbed the atmosphere of the city through the soles of his shoes. Occasionally he attended the theater or a concert. For the most part, however, he guarded his meager funds carefully and limited his luxuries to the purchase of books.

Early in September, Vladimir was on his way back to St. Petersburg. At the border the Russian police examined his luggage carefully and passed him through. He breathed a sigh of relief. They had failed to spot the hectograph—a gelatin pad used for printing multiple copies—and the illegal literature which he had carefully concealed in the false bottom of his trunk.

6.

Siberian Journey

AFTER A SUMMER abroad, Vladimir found it hard to pick up the threads of life in St. Petersburg once more. He was also plagued with personal problems. Since revolutionary activity left him less and less time to earn a living, he was increasingly dependent on his mother for money. As a result, though he and Nadezhda loved each other, marriage was out of the question.

The political picture in Russia was also frustrating. In the months he had been away it had changed—so much so that the Marxists were immobilized by confusion and disunity. Their uncertainty stemmed from the ascension to the throne of twenty-six-year-old Tsar Nicholas II on the death of his father Alexander III the previous fall. Harsh, uncompromising Alexander had been a perfect focal point for the hostility and propaganda of Russian radicalism. But young Tsar Nicholas did not offer quite so easy a target. Although indecisive and weak-willed, he was at the same time charming and well intentioned. Accordingly, he had managed to achieve a degree of personal popularity with the masses.

Politically, Nicholas was a conservative. He warned the Russian people against "senseless dreams" of radical reform. Nevertheless, he acquired a few liberal advisers who saw the need for some economic and social improvements. Shortly after he came to the throne, programs of commercial growth and industrial expansion were announced. Many people came to associate Russia's rapid recovery from the depression of two years before with Nicholas' assumption of power.

In addition, some of the government's more repressive policies were eased. While the police censors still held their jobs, they were directed to be more lenient. Many liberal writings which had been banned under Alexander III were now permitted to see print. Even Marxist literature was frequently passed by the censors, provided it was couched in nonmilitant academic language. A sort of game developed among radical authors to see how far they could go in publishing revolutionary doctrines disguised as scholarly studies.

The change in official policy perplexed Vladimir as well as his fellow revolutionaries. On the one hand, he welcomed the relaxation of censorship because it made it easier to disseminate Marxist ideas. But he was also mindful that a revolutionary movement needed villains to attack. And a more relaxed government policy made it harder to paint the Tsar as an unreconstructed enemy of the people.

He corresponded secretly with George Plekhanov and Paul Axelrod in Switzerland to report on developments and seek their guidance. The letters were hidden in the bindings of innocuous books to elude the police censors. But the political situation in Russia was so complex and changeable that it was impossible to work out an effective strategy by mail.

However, in the fall of 1895 there were new and unforeseen developments that promised to give Lenin and others who shared his views a new lease on life. Economic progress and greater individual freedom had combined to engender new hope in the Russian people. The working masses, glimpsing a better future for themselves, were increasingly impatient to throw off the remaining shackles of repression that had bound them for so long. In St. Petersburg a wave of illegal strikes broke out spontaneously in many of the large factories. They were aimed at achieving improved working conditions and better wages.

Vladimir shrewdly saw in the strikes the opportunity the Marxists had been waiting for. He and his fellow revolutionaries immediately swung into action to try to exploit the strikes for their own ends. Militant handbills were secretly hectographed and distributed, calling on workers to fight not only for improved factory conditions but for "socialism and freedom." Although some of the leaflets were seized by factory foremen and turned over to the police, others passed surreptitiously from hand to hand among strikers and non-strikers.

As a leader among the agitators, Vladimir tutored the less experienced radicals in various techniques of underground activity. He showed them how to use codes, mix invisible inks and evade the police.

The tireless Vladimir also drew up plans for an underground newspaper to be entitled *The Worker's Cause*. It was to be printed on a secret press belonging to a rival group of radicals. Although Vladimir had denounced them bitterly in the past, the rival organization agreed to bury their differences for the moment in order to help the striking workers.

In addition to serving as editor of *The Worker's Cause,* Vladimir wrote most of the articles for the initial number. One night in December, just as the first issue was about to go to press, a squad of police burst into Vladimir's lodgings and placed him under arrest. A search of his rooms produced copies of underground literature. He was taken down to the police station and questioned. What was he doing with illegal pamphlets and books? Was he a member of a revolutionary group?

Vladimir explained that he had innocently accepted the illicit reading matter from some passerby whom he had never seen before. He calmly denied being a revolutionary. After several hours of grilling the police threw him into a small cell in the St. Petersburg House of Detention.

At first, Vladimir was confident that he would be released in short order. He was convinced the police had no real evidence and were merely out to intimidate him. But as the days passed and he was not freed, he began to fear his case was more serious than he had thought.

He requested permission to correspond with friends and relatives outside. To his surprise, the prison warders made no objection. He wrote to Nadezhda, his mother and members of the movement. On lines he inserted invisible messages in milk. When heated over a the surface the letters were innocuous enough. But in between the candle flame, the words turned yellowish brown. It was one of the techniques he had taught his fellow revolutionaries, and now he desperately hoped they would remember it. They did. In reply he received milk messages containing full information on what had happened.

As it turned out, the police had planted a spy in their midst—a dentist named Dr. Mikhailov—whom the radicals had trusted. From him the authorities had learned all about the illegal agitation at the industrial plants. In addition to Vladimir, the police had taken half a dozen other leading Marxists into custody. Miraculously, Nadezhda had escaped arrest.

Shortly after Dr. Mikhailov's role as a police agent was made known within the revolutionary movement, he was found murdered. His killers remained undiscovered.

Vladimir learned he could borrow books from the outside while in jail. He was jubilant. Books not only provided mental nourishment but served as auxiliary means of communicating secretly when milk was not available. This was done by marking tiny dots in certain letters on selected pages. When the letters were combined, they formed words and sentences. But he relied on the milk method as often as possible, for it was simpler and less eye-wearying. He used part of his bread supply to knead hollow pellets to hold the milk. When he heard a guard approach, he quickly swallowed the pellets. In one secret message, he wryly explained to a correspondent, "Today, I have eaten six inkpots."

To protect his valuable letter-writing and book-borrowing privileges, Vladimir behaved like a model prisoner. He did as he was told, and cooperated with the guards in every way. In return, they treated him with extreme consideration. And occasionally they even allowed him to have limited contact with other prisoners.

As a means of keeping fit, he did calisthenics in his cell every day. Curiously enough, though the cell was small, cold and poorly ventilated, he did not really feel confined at all. It was not unlike being shut up in a monastery. For perhaps the first time in his life, he had a sense of complete release from worldly responsibilities. Therefore, every waking moment could be devoted to thinking about Marxism and revolution.

He set to work on a monumental study of the development of capitalism in Russia, after receiving approval from prison officials. At the same time he wrote numerous militant statements on revolution which he smuggled out, using the milk technique. These were reproduced by his friends outside and distributed by the hundreds in St. Petersburg and elsewhere. The police, he learned, had gotten their hands on some of the pamphlets and were searching in vain for the anonymous author. "I'm in a far better position than most of the citizens in Russia," he wrote triumphantly in one secret message to a correspondent. "They can never find me."

As the months passed, Vladimir's writings from within the jail began to exert a growing influence on Marxists all over Russia. Thus, he was more influential in Cell 193 of the St. Petersburg House of Detention than he had ever been on the outside!

In February of 1897, a year and a month after his arrest, Vladimir was finally discharged from jail. But he was not free. The provisions of his release called for him to be exiled to Siberia for a period of three years.

Given less than a week to prepare for his journey, he and Nadezhda took the train to Moscow to spend time with his family. "It's a pity they let us out so soon," he told his sister Anna almost regretfully. "I should have liked to do a little more work on the book. It will prove difficult to get books in Siberia."

Nevertheless, Vladimir soon accepted the prospect of banishment to Siberia with the same equanimity he had shown toward his imprisonment. In truth, he began to view it with the cheerfulness of an adventurer about to embark on an exciting journey. His mother and Nadezhda grieved quietly at the thought of a long separation. But Vladimir assured them repeatedly that there was no cause for sadness. He would manage as well in Siberia as he had in jail, he declared serenely.

Actually, he had good reason to feel confident. He had learned from fellow radicals who had recently returned from Siberia that the life of a political exile was not at all hard or difficult. In terms of personal freedom, it was a great improvement over prison. The brutal beatings and killings that once had been the accepted lot of exiles were no longer permitted. True, there were still prisons in

Siberia staffed by tough, tyrannical guards; but such places were used to house common criminals convicted of murder or other heinous crimes. A political exile, on the other hand, fell into a different category. Since he was not a prisoner in the usual sense, he was free to live as he wished. The government furnished him with a small allowance to cover the basic cost of his room, board and other necessities. The exile could obtain lodgings with a private family or even rent a house of his own, if he had additional private funds. He could correspond freely, write books, go hunting—there was no ban on owning a gun!—or travel anywhere within the local region.

The restrictions that did exist were minor ones. An exile was forbidden to enter a large city, even within the area of his confinement. He was also subject to periodic visits from a police inspector. But these were petty annoyances which most exiles did not view as real hardships.

Thus Vladimir had little reason to consider his banishment a tragedy. Rather, he saw it in pragmatic terms as a splendid opportunity for the leisure and serenity he required to make bold revolutionary plans for the future.

Even at the Moscow station, while boarding the train that was to carry him to his far destination, Vladimir was in good spirits. He kissed his mother, sisters and Nadezhda good-bye, embraced his brother Dmitry and Mark Elisarov and promised wryly that he would see them all in a few years. As the train chugged slowly out of the terminal, he waved and smiled as if he were on his way to a day's outing in the country.

Vladimir was well prepared to cope with life in Siberia. In addition to a trunk full of warm clothing, he had more than a hundred books and boxes of notes and manuscript pages from his projected history of Russian capitalism. Furthermore, he had a thousand rubles which his mother had given him to supplement his government allowance. With the pleasant prospect of completing a major piece of writing and sufficient funds to assure himself of reasonable comfort, he felt he had no reason for complaint.

To go from Moscow to the city of Krasnoyarsk in the center of the great Siberian plain was a journey of two thousand miles and eleven days. The train crept past tiny villages and broad fields inhabited by herds of small sad-eyed goats. It snaked through the rolling Ural Mountains, emerging finally onto the mighty ice-covered Siberian steppes. To Vladimir, staring out of the soot-covered train window, Siberia was a single vast ocean of dazzling white. Occasionally, off in the distance, a stand of majestic evergreens broke the line of the horizon like an island in a frozen sea.

Since he was traveling without guards, he was free to meet and talk with the other passengers. One or two proved to be political exiles like himself, and with them he formed a particularly close bond. However, most of his time was spent in reading, jotting down notes for his book or gazing out at the scenery.

When the train finally rumbled into the station at Krasnoyarsk, Vladimir was surprised to find it a city of some size. He had expected a backward, rural outpost. Instead, he found a thriving urban community complete with municipal library, fine shops and even a place where he could pick up two-week-old Moscow newspapers.

In St. Petersburg he had been told to proceed to Krasnoyarsk and await further orders there. But he discovered that the police in the Siberian city had received no instructions. Since they did not know what to do with him and the other exiles who had just arrived, Vladimir lived in perfect freedom for the next two months. He rented a room in Krasnoyarsk and spent most of his time in the library or taking long walks. He even obtained a temporary job working as a librarian with the private collection of a millionaire merchant!

Finally, with the coming of Siberia's torrential rains in April, Vladimir's orders arrived. He was to proceed to the village of Shushenskoye, some two hundred miles south of Krasnoyarsk.

The journey was by steamer, a pleasant leisurely voyage down the Yenisei River. The trip took a week. Shushenskoye was a tiny rural community in fertile flatlands hard by a fragrant game-filled forest and streams teeming with fish. In spite of the cruel Siberian winters, the other seasons in this southern part of the country were mild and pleasant. As a result, Vladimir could not help feeling that the region had most of the characteristics of a rustic vacation retreat rather than a place of exile.

In Shushenskoye, he reported to the local constable, an informal, good-natured official. The policeman merely noted in his record book that his charge had arrived, then announced that he was free to live and go where he liked. Vladimir obtained lodgings with a well-to-do peasant named Apollon Zyrianov, who charged him eight rubles a month for room, meals and laundry. Compared to the prices in St. Petersburg and Moscow, the cost of living in Shushenskoye was astonishingly low. Vladimir realized with a start that the thousand rubles his mother had given him, plus his exile's allowance, made him one of the wealthiest men in the region!

The first months in Shushenskoye were like an extended vacation. His gruff, good-natured peasant-landlord liked him and took him hunting and fishing almost daily. Zyrianov even built shelves for his books, although that was not part of their rental agreement.

Since there were exiles in other villages within a fifty-mile radius, there was a good deal of visiting back and forth. Sometimes several agreed to meet at a central point to discuss political philosophy and revolutionary strategy. But just as often Vladimir arranged to meet a fellow exile simply to go hunting or hiking. On such occasions Marxism was forgotten as they went out into the forest with fowling pieces under their arms. Vladimir still retained a strong aversion to killing game. But he did enjoy the challenge of tracking down an animal as well as the serenity of the forest itself.

Every postal delivery brought books, newspapers and letters from home. His mother and Nadezhda wrote regularly, evincing grave concern for his welfare in "a savage and primitive" land. Vladimir, growing plump on hearty peasant meals and a leisurely routine, replied bravely that conditions in Siberia were not as bad as they thought.

Life was so enjoyable that Vladimir did almost no serious work during the first months. He read, but did little writing except for several pamphlets which were smuggled to his friends in St. Petersburg through the usual milk-ink method. These were reprinted in quantity and distributed as had been his writings from prison. On Sundays he set up an unofficial law office to which the *muzhiks,* or peasants, came from miles around for free legal advice. Vladimir counseled them on collecting unpaid wages and arbitrated petty disputes between neighbors or relatives.

By fall, Vladimir decided to shake himself out of his torpor and get to work in earnest. He began to pour out a regular stream of book reviews and articles on economics and sociology. He employed a restrained and scholarly style so that they would be approved by the censor for legal publication. These writings were sold to magazines which paid him up to two hundred rubles for a single article. He also arranged with publishers in Moscow and St. Petersburg to serve them as a professional translator of foreign works to be published in Russian. Pleased with the commercial rewards of authorship, Vladimir plunged wholeheartedly into completing *The Development of Capitalism in Russia*. Even before the manuscript was completed, he arranged by correspondence for its sale to a publisher for fifteen hundred rubles!

As the long winter months set in and snow piled high against the doors and windows of Zyrianov's house, Vladimir began to feel isolated from the real world. His sense of loneliness, submerged during the idyllic summer and autumn, began to gnaw at him. He fought it as best he could by completely burying himself in his work.

In mid-March, a "congress" of Russian Marxists was held in the city of Minsk. The participants proclaimed the founding of a new political party—the Russian Social Democratic Party. Until now, the most important radical group had been the Social Revolutionary Party, whose members had led terrorist raids against landowners in the rural areas. The Social Revolutionaries claimed that the nation would be led to Marxism through the Russian peasants. The new Social Democratic Party was formed as a rival group, pledged to overthrow the Tsar and establish socialism through the factory workers. Since it advocated his particular brand of Marxism, Vladimir was delighted to learn of its formation.

One day, ominous news from Moscow penetrated the cold, deadly Siberian winter. A letter from his mother informed Vladimir that Nadezhda had been arrested in St. Petersburg! It was particularly jarring because there had been not the slightest hint that Nadezhda had fallen under suspicion. Later, he learned through secret messages from revolutionary friends that she and several other female party members had actually been under police surveillance for many months.

Vladimir was informed that after a brief stay in the House of Detention, Nadezhda would be exiled for three years in Ufa, a region in the southern Urals. He immediately wrote back suggesting how she might be able to join him. Nadezhda was to have a lawyer petition the government to permit her to go to her "fiancé" in Shushenskoye so that they could be married.

The plan succeeded. The government approved the request. But Nadezhda was warned that if she and Vladimir were not married immediately, she would be sent to Ufa after all.

One day in May of 1898 Nadezhda left St. Petersburg for the long journey to Siberia. She was accompanied by her mother, Elizabeth Krupskaya. They carried a good deal of luggage, but some of it consisted of minor luxuries that Vladimir had requested which were in short supply in Shushenskoye. He had asked for stationery, penwipers, scissors, a chess set and other items. But mainly he wanted books and more books, including such reference works as a dictionary and grammar to help him in his writing and translation work.

Their arrival in sleepy Shushenskoye was a major event. The news spread rapidly throughout the village and for miles beyond. Vladimir embraced Nadezhda and confessed that he had missed her. His stately, aristocratic mother-in-law-to-be examined him with a critical eye and announced that he had put on too much weight.

Nadezhda did not like the Zyrianov family. She felt they drank too much, were coarse-mannered and far too inquisitive. Could they not rent a house instead of rooms? she asked Vladimir. He made inquiries and found a house where he could lease a whole wing for only four rubles a month.

Nadezhda was delighted and urged him to close the deal immediately. He did. She and her mother set to work putting their new home in spotless order. She even planted a garden so they could have their own fresh vegetables.

In spite of these preparations, official red tape delayed their marriage for weeks. Vladimir learned to his amazement that although he had been in Siberia for more than a year, the constable had not yet received his government file from the capital! Without these documents, a marriage certificate could not be issued to him. The papers finally arrived in July. They were married on July 22, 1898, by the village notary.

With his new wife and mother-in-law looking after the household, Vladimir returned to his books and notes. Most of his time was spent completing his big work on Russian capitalism. But he was not too preoccupied to follow political developments in Moscow and St. Petersburg closely. What he read gave him the feeling that Russia was changing and he was no longer a part of it. From newspapers and letters, he learned that the economic boom was continuing. He also discovered that the workers in the factories were conducting successful strikes for increased wages and improved working conditions. Furthermore, they were achieving their gains by following grass-roots leadership developed in their own ranks, not by rallying behind the revolutionists of the Social Democratic Party. Vladimir was dismayed by these developments; they appeared to indicate that Russia was moving away from revolution instead of toward it.

There was no denying that these were hard times for Russian radicalism. Vladimir felt that a critical factor was the lack of sound Marxist leadership. Most dedicated leaders were, like himself, either in jail or exiled.

By the start of his third year in Siberia he had lost his earlier equanimity. Sick at heart at the discouraging news from outside, he was no longer serene about his forced stay in Siberia. In this hour of crisis, when the sinking revolutionary movement needed him most, he was helplessly shut away in Shushenskoye. By now he had finished writing his book on Russian capitalism and had sent the manuscript to the publisher. It was a major achievement and should have given him satisfaction—but it did not. The tranquil life devoid of responsibility which he had once relished now left a taste of bitterness and guilt.

Nadezhda could do nothing with him. He became preoccupied and moody, given to sudden fits of temper. Sometimes he walked for hours alone in the forest; at other times he paced tensely back and forth in his room like a helpless, imprisoned tiger. He grew indifferent to food and lost a great deal of weight.

Yet what outwardly seemed merely pique and frustration actually masked an involved process of internal deliberation. Vladimir believed that unless drastic measures were taken, the Marxist movement in Russia was doomed. What was needed most of all, he felt, was a new battle plan for the war against capitalism. He was convinced that the troubles of the Social Democratic Party stemmed from its own internal weakness. The writings of Marx and Engels had provided it with a philosophy, but a sound structure and a cohesive strategy were missing. The Social Democratic Party's lack of professional leadership was freezing it into inaction. Most of its members were well-meaning but poorly trained amateurs for whom revolutionary activity was a kind of hobby or game.

Vladimir was certain that successful revolutions were not planned and carried through by amateurs. What was needed, he felt, were trained, experienced leaders for whom revolutionary activity was a way of life.

Soon a plan began to unfold in his mind—a plan so simple, yet so audacious in concept that its implications were staggering! *Revolutions must be waged like wars—by massive armies under the unified direction of a central corps of trained disciplined leaders.* The leadership must be restricted to professional revolutionaries. They would educate, organize and train followers while deciding all matters of strategy and tactics. Once they issued orders, these must be accepted and obeyed without doubt or dissent in the ranks.

Moreover, until the revolutionary movement was strong enough to assert itself, its operations would have to be kept secret. Accordingly, the initial organization must be conspiratorial in nature, small in size and highly centralized. Membership would be restricted to a group of select leaders whose lives were completely dedicated to Marxism and revolution. A key instrument of the movement would be an all-Russian underground newspaper which would be smuggled into cities and factories and across frontiers by its secret members.

Vladimir saw his plan as indispensable to realizing the goals of Marxism. He also recognized in the plan a major role for himself. While Karl Marx had been the prophet and spiritual leader of revolution, he, Vladimir Ulyanov, would provide the practical organization to carry it through. It was a dizzying thought.

7.

The Exile

VLADIMIR'S EXILE was to end in January 1900. Since Nadezhda's term still had a year to go, he had to make a choice. He could either remain in Shushenskoye with her or return to the west alone. If he chose to leave her, she would have to serve out her final year in Ufa, the region to which she had been assigned originally.

To Vladimir the decision was obvious. Consumed by Marxist fervor and a need to promote his plan of organization, he made up his mind to leave Shushenskoye. Nadezhda, faithful to her role as the wife of a revolutionary, did not voice any objection. She appeared to accept the notion that her husband's duty to the movement came ahead of anything else.

One cold winter afternoon Vladimir, Nadezhda and her mother packed all their belongings in a covered sleigh and headed north along the frozen Yenisei River. Their destination was Krasnoyarsk, two hundred miles away, where they would begin the long rail journey west. Vladimir's plan was to stop briefly at Ufa to help Nadezhda and her mother get settled. Then he would proceed the rest of the way home alone.

Bursting with impatience, Vladimir urged the sleigh driver to go faster. He even fumed at the brief delays at the stagehouses to change horses and use the rest facilities. Day and night they drove on relentlessly. By day the reflected sun turned the snow-blanketed countryside into a blinding sea of gold. At night, in the soft light of the full moon, it was transformed into a magical ocean of silver and frost-white.

The air was piercingly cold. Nadezhda and her mother huddled in their fur coats to protect themselves against the biting weather. Vladimir, however, did not even bother to wear his overcoat, for he was so preoccupied that he was scarcely aware of the freezing temperature.

In Krasnoyarsk, they took the first train west to Ufa. Vladimir's stopover in the Ural province was brief, just long enough to help his wife and mother-in-law move into decent lodgings. Then he headed west again toward Moscow and St. Petersburg.

In Moscow he received a tearful welcome from his mother and sisters. They urged him to remain but he pleaded that his business could not wait and he must get to the capital at once. According to police regulations, he was allowed to stay anywhere except in St. Petersburg itself. So he chose the small town of Pskov, a rail junction close to the Latvian border, only a hundred miles from the capital. It was an ideal location for smuggling in contraband literature as well as for sneaking into St. Petersburg in disguise.

Upon settling in the town, Vladimir tried to give the impression that he was done with politics. He met many of the influential residents and indicated he was now only interested in a legal career. His real purpose, of course, was to develop a false "cover" in order to mislead the police who, he knew, were keeping him under surveillance. One of the persons with whom he became friendly was a Prince Obolensky, the most important man in Pskov. With the Prince's help, he managed to obtain a passport enabling him to travel abroad—a precious possession for a former exile.

Vladimir's secret operations were something else again. He hurled himself into underground activity like a thirsty traveler coming upon an oasis in the desert. He made regular trips to St. Petersburg with illegal literature, using different disguises and indirect routes to outwit the police.

Vladimir learned that the Social Democrats in the capital were disheartened by the way things were going. He spoke to them impassionedly about reorganizing the party but did not elicit much encouragement. It was only when he outlined his plan for a revolutionary newspaper that there was a genuine burst of enthusiasm. A publication, after all, was a tangible and immediate undertaking to which a party member could harness his energy in the hope of seeing quick results.

News of the project got to George Plekhanov in Switzerland. He sent Vera Zasulich, a trusted deputy, to a secret rendezvous in St. Petersburg to discuss the plan with Vladimir and the others. Everybody agreed that an underground newspaper could serve as a first spark in firing up a new revolutionary spirit. Someone suggested that it be called *Iskra*—"the Spark." The name received unanimous approval. Initial financing was to come from a wealthy woman sympathizer named Alexandra Kalmykova, known affectionately within the movement as "Auntie." "Auntie" had promised two thousand rubles.

It was understood that the paper was to be edited by Vladimir and two other former exiles with whom he had become friendly— Jules Martov and Alexander Potresov. While in exile the three had maintained a regular correspondence and seemed to be in close political accord.

Vladimir and his associates spent the next few weeks carefully planning the editorial structure and format. One day in early June he and Martov set out from Pskov to meet contacts in St. Petersburg. They carried illegal literature as well as lists of addresses written in invisible ink on unimposing scraps of paper. Arriving in the capital, they went to the home of a sympathizer on Kazachy Street to spend the night.

The next morning, just as they left the house, they were suddenly surrounded by police. Arrested and taken to jail, they were searched and interrogated. But the police did not carefully examine the old receipts and other scraps of paper found on the prisoners. They appeared concerned mainly with Vladimir's and Martov's violation of police rules against entering the forbidden city. The inspector chuckled at their clumsy efforts to evade surveillance. He warned them that in spite of their roundabout route they could not escape the eye of the police. To prove his point he ticked off on his fingers the various places where they had changed trains.

Vladimir and Martov were kept in jail for two weeks. Then they were suddenly released with no explanation given. The police even returned Vladimir's precious passport, which he had feared would be confiscated.

It was clear that they could no longer remain in Russia. Since the police seemed able to keep track of their whereabouts virtually every minute of the day, underground activity had become impossible. But where to go?

They agreed that the obvious answer was Switzerland, where Plekhanov, Axelrod and the other exiled leaders lived. First, however, Vladimir wanted to see his wife in Ufa. To get permission for him to do so, his mother interceded once more with the government. Authorization for the visit was granted on condition that Madame Ulyanov accompany her son to Ufa to guarantee his behavior.

In late June, Vladimir, his mother and his sister Anna left Moscow by train for the thousand-mile journey east. Maria Alexandrovna was by now a small, white-haired woman in her early sixties whose face bespoke years of anguish. In addition to her concern for Vladimir she also worried on behalf of her youngest son and daughter. Both Dmitry, now a twenty-six-year-old physician, and Maria, twenty-two, had recently been jailed for radical activity. Although their mother had managed to obtain their release, it was clear that they were on their way to following in Vladimir's footsteps.

The week in Ufa was used by Vladimir to political advantage. He was reunited with Nadezhda and spent a good deal of time with her. But he also circulated among the other exiles and distributed a secret code he had devised. The code, he explained, would be used for revolutionary correspondence after he was abroad.

A month later, Vladimir left Russia. It was not a happy departure, for he knew full well that he might never see his homeland again. He went directly to Geneva to work out with Plekhanov and others the final plans for the publication of *Iskra*. Expecting to find an atmosphere of warmth, cooperation and accord, he was shocked to discover the exiled leaders deeply divided. Cool, elegant Plekhanov, legendary hero of the youthful revolutionaries, appeared resentful of the newer leaders. A nasty quarrel over the newspaper ensued, with Vladimir serving as spokesman for the younger

Marxists. He saw in *Iskra* a practical tool for reorganizing the Social Democratic Party. Plekhanov, the theorist, argued for an "elevated tone." He wanted a publication in which bread-and-butter questions of organizational strategy and tactics would be subordinated to theoretical issues.

At one point the wrangle took a bitter, personal turn. Vladimir had written an editorial statement for the first issue in which he outlined the aims of the new publication. Plekhanov criticized it for lack of "literary quality." The younger Marxist was deeply hurt and indignant.

The feud finally ended in a negotiated truce. An editorial board of six was set up to determine policy. It consisted of Vladimir, Plekhanov, Axelrod, Vera Zasulich, Jules Martov and Alexander Potresov. But it was obvious to all that relations between Plekhanov and Vladimir had been permanently strained.

To minimize Plekhanov's influence on *Iskra*, Vladimir arranged to have the newspaper printed in Germany. He himself moved to Munich to be near the printer. Martov and Vera Zasulich also went to Munich. As a result, Plekhanov had to vote on editorial decisions by mail from Geneva. Vladimir also took control of the underground distribution of the publication, which gave him a link to the key Social Democrats in Russia.

When Nadezhda completed her term at Ufa, she joined her husband in Munich. Vladimir strengthened his hand against Plekhanov still further by getting the editorial board to appoint her secretary of *Iskra*.

Having successfully outmaneuvered the older Marxist, he now began to use the publication as a personal vehicle. A tireless worker, he wrote article after article for the paper. Some issues contained several long essays by him. At first he used a variety of pseudonyms or simply initials. Among them were "Illyin" or "V. Illyin," derived from his middle name Ilyich. Searching for a variation that would be easier to pronounce and to remember, he finally hit on the pseudonym "Lenin." He enjoyed the sound and simplicity of it. From that time on, all of his writings would be signed either "Lenin" or "V. I. Lenin." It was important to him to make the name so well known through his written works that it would be readily recognized in radical circles. He reasoned that in order to assume an even stronger leadership role he needed greater stature. During the quarrel over *Iskra*, Plekhanov had contemptuously criticized his lack of credentials as an originator of ideas. Now he set out to correct this deficiency. His recently published book, *The Development of Capitalism in Russia,* was already enjoying an influential circulation. The articles in *Iskra,* supplemented by the earlier pamphlets he had written, gave him added prestige.

In a short time, Vladimir completely dominated the new paper. The name "Lenin" was soon passing from mouth to mouth in underground circles. His special style and point of view were easily distinguishable to the regular readers of *Iskra*. They began to talk of Lenin with affection and respect. When Russian exiles went abroad, they now asked to meet him in much the same way that he himself had once sought out George Plekhanov.

The key emphasis in Lenin's writings was on the practical application of revolutionary strategy. To him, theoretical issues were only a means to an end. He was out to create a party—to unify all the scattered local Social Democratic study and discussion circles into a single action movement. And he meant to accomplish this through *Iskra*.

The paper proved to be not only a means of communication but a school for professional revolutionists as well. According to the organization plan Lenin had formulated, the leaders of the party were to be a small, highly disciplined group of conspirators. The staff of secret agents which he began to recruit for *Iskra* was the nucleus of such an elite. In Russia they spied out information for the paper, kept a watchful eye on public opinion and did effective propaganda work. They also set up machinery for smuggling copies of *Iskra* into the country and distributing it in every important city. Because the paper's staff was small, organization and discipline were required. With every issue, the organizational techniques were improved. The *Iskra* agents perfected evasion methods, established secret routes and carefully recruited additional workers. And the dominating spirit of the entire enterprise was Lenin himself.

In articles written for the early issues, Vladimir began to outline his organizational blueprint for revolution. In the very first number he set down the two basic principles of his plan:

(1) *Without the guidance of the elite revolutionaries, the laboring classes would become "petty and inevitably bourgeois";*
(2) *The "socialist vanguard" would be composed of people "who shall devote to the revolution not only their spare evenings, but the whole of their lives."*

The concept of an elite group of leaders was actually a radical departure from basic Marxist doctrine. Marx and Engels had written: "The emancipation of the working class is the work of the working class itself." They had held that the task of Communists was to teach workers to understand the nature of their plight, not to lead them.

Lenin, however, was a Marxist who was above all a pragmatist. His concern at this point was with the organization of the revolution rather than its philosophy. Through the establishment of a select leadership, he saw a practical approach to the task of making the revolution. For him the effectiveness of such a strategy outweighed the violence done to Marxist theory. Where Marx wrote of the working class emancipating itself, Lenin saw the emancipation being led by a revolutionary core who would seize power *in the name of the masses.*

But Lenin failed to deal with some basic issues. How would the revolutionary leaders be chosen? How would they know what was best for the proletariat? Once in power, would they ever turn this power over to the proletariat? These were questions he deliberately thrust aside because he himself did not yet have the answers.

In May of 1901, Lenin set to work on a small book in which he elaborated on his *Iskra* articles. He called it *What's to Be Done?* Just as the *Communist Manifesto* had become the bible of Marxist doctrine, he foresaw his work as becoming a key manual on the organization of the revolution.

In *What's to Be Done?* Lenin wrote in ruthlessly logical and unyielding terms. He pointed out that only those groups that were prepared to surrender their autonomy could be accepted into the revolutionary movement. Any group that was not ready to submit to the central direction of the organization would be excluded.

He also declared that the immediate needs of the working class must be subordinated to the interests of the general revolutionary struggle against tsarism. He had good reason for emphasizing this point. Lenin himself had little faith in the revolutionary zeal of the masses. He had warned in his first article in *Iskra* that peasants and workers tended to become "petty and bourgeois" without revolutionary leaders. Thus, he feared that if left to themselves they would prefer immediate material gains to a real revolution. They would expend their efforts on seeking better wages, hours and factory conditions. Long-range political goals would be subordinated to these narrower economic objectives. He speculated that a shrewd tsar might even encourage such labor reforms precisely in order to divert the workers' energies from the true revolutionary struggle.

Lenin anticipated the development of powerful worker-run unions that would be concerned primarily with improving labor conditions. He foresaw that such groups, rather than the "true revolutionary leadership," would have first call on the loyalty of the working class.

For these reasons Lenin was convinced that the improvement of the worker's lot and the development of effective labor unions must be subordinated to the basic political struggle against the Tsar. "Economism"—the emphasis on material gains—must be ruthlessly suppressed, he argued, and those who advocated it must be branded enemies of the revolution.

The heart of *What's to Be Done?* was a powerfully blunt reiteration of Lenin's basic concept of revolutionary organization:

> I assert: 1. that no movement can be durable without a stable organization of leaders to maintain continuity; 2. that the more widely the masses are drawn into the struggle and form the basis of the movement, the more it is necessary to have such an organization and the more stable it must be; 3. that the organization must consist chiefly of persons engaged in revolution as a profession; 4. that in a country with a despotic government, the more we *restrict* the membership of this organization to those who are engaged in revolution as a profession . . . the more difficult it will

be to catch the organization; and 5. the *wider* will be the circle of men and women of the working class or of other classes of society able to join the movement and perform active work in it.

Lenin had begun formulating his general principles in Siberia. But it was only in the process of trying to set them down on paper that he was able to think through their detailed application. And in the work of creating his comprehensive blueprint for revolution, Lenin also underwent an ordeal of self-discovery. In content and tone *What's to Be Done?* was as blunt and uncompromising as Lenin himself. It was an amazingly accurate mirror of its author's personality as well as his mind.

The manuscript was published in Stuttgart, Germany, in March 1902. Lenin was only thirty-one at the time; yet the book's contents were to serve as his political guiding star for the next twenty years.

Shortly after *What's to Be Done?* was off the press, Lenin and his fellow editors of *Iskra* were faced with a crisis. The German firm that had been printing the newspaper suddenly decided that it was too dangerous a venture. They feared their association with a revolutionary paper would alienate their other customers and get them into trouble with the German government. Consequently they canceled the printing agreement without notice.

A hasty meeting of the editorial board was called. There was intensive debate as to where to move the *Iskra* headquarters. Plekhanov and Axelrod argued that it should be in Switzerland. Lenin, intent on staying as far away from Plekhanov's influence as possible, insisted they would have greater freedom of action in England. His point of view prevailed. A majority of the board finally voted in favor of moving the editorial office to London.

When Lenin and Nadezhda arrived in the English capital the city was enveloped in dense fog. But when the blanket lifted they found a metropolis more cosmopolitan than any they had ever visited before. While astonished by the sheer size of London, Lenin soon fell in love with it. He was especially taken with the museums, libraries and parks, where he began to spend most of his spare time when not working on *Iskra*.

There was a large colony of Russian revolutionary exiles in London, and Lenin soon established a close relationship with many of them. Through one of the exiles he and Nadezhda managed to rent a two-room apartment in Holford Square for thirty shillings a month. It was small and unimposing, but it was a place to sleep and work and there was a gas jet for cooking their modest meals.

Lenin set about the task of learning to speak English with his usual determination. He insisted that everyone converse with him in English only. On Sundays he visited Hyde Park where outdoor speakers congregated. He did not listen to what they had to say but concentrated on their lip movements in order to improve his pronunciation.

Jules Martov and Vera Zasulich came from Munich to help with the editing. As the months went by, scarcely an issue went to press without sharp debate and angry words. Though in Switzerland, Plekhanov wrote many letters critical of Lenin's articles. At this point he and Lenin were barely civil to each other in their correspondence. The conflict affected Lenin's relationship with Martov and Vera Zasulich as well. Both had great affection for Plekhanov and shared his aversion to dogmatic inflexibility on political issues. Lenin's harsh, uncompromising approach created a growing schism. Martov finally grew so disgusted that he packed up and returned to the continent. Lenin thus found himself in opposition to everyone else on the editorial board.

One autumn morning there was a knock on the door of the apartment on Holford Street. The visitor was a young man with a large head of wavy hair, deep, penetrating eyes and a pleasant, modulated voice. His real name was Lev Davydovich Bronstein, but his passport, which was forged, was in the name of "Leon Trotsky." At twenty-two this son of a poor farmer was already a hard-core veteran of the Social Democratic underground, and had recently escaped from Siberian exile.

Known in the underground as "the Pen," Bronstein (or Trotsky) was a youth with an amazingly agile mind. He wrote and spoke brilliantly. But he and Lenin proved to be as different as night and day. Charming and outgoing, Trotsky loved to talk while Lenin, self-contained almost to the point of dourness, did most of the listening. Nevertheless, the younger man soon got on the right side of Lenin by heaping outrageous flattery on *The Development of Capitalism in Russia*. Thereafter they rarely saw each other socially. Yet Lenin felt that once the revolution came, there would be an important role in it for the youth. He nominated Trotsky to the *Iskra* board. But the move was sharply opposed by Plekhanov, who was not about to place an ally of Lenin's in such a strategic spot.

The conflict among the *Iskra* editors went from bad to worse. The paper itself had been an instant success; revolutionaries throughout Russia were clamoring for more copies. Yet if the split continued, it was doubtful that *Iskra* could go on at all.

In the spring of 1903, Plekhanov convinced the board that it was absurd to publish the paper from London when half the editors were in Switzerland. Over Lenin's vigorous opposition, the board decided to move the editorial offices to Geneva, Plekhanov's home ground. Lenin took this defeat so badly that he found himself on the verge of physical and mental collapse. A nervous disorder resulted in severe inflammation of his back and chest. In an attempt to relieve his discomfort, Nadezhda applied iodine to the afflicted area. The medication only made the pain more excruciating.

In April 1903, with his back and chest still on fire, Lenin and his wife packed their belongings and left London for Geneva. He felt the time had come for a direct confrontation between himself and Plekhanov to determine who would dominate *Iskra* and the Social Democratic Party.

8.

Bolsheviks and Mensheviks

IN GENEVA the Lenins moved into a small, drab house in a working-class district. Since there was no money to buy furniture, Nadezhda used the wooden packing cases in which they had shipped Vladimir's books from London as tables and chairs.

Meanwhile Lenin prepared for the inevitable showdown with Plekhanov. He felt it would come during the summer, when the Social Democratic Party was to hold its second Congress in Brussels, Belgium. The first Congress, which had taken place in Minsk in 1898 while Lenin was in exile, had seen the formation of the party.

The Brussels meeting was held in an empty, rundown warehouse which had been festooned with bright red crepe. The Social Democrats were told by speakers recently in Russia that discontent was widespread. They heard reports of peasant uprisings, industrial strikes and pogroms. The government was increasingly alienated from the people, according to these accounts.

During the early speeches, Lenin was intensely active behind the scenes lining up support for his expected clash with Plekhanov. Yet when the fight came, he was astonished to find his opposition coming from an unexpected quarter.

The initial conflict stemmed from a dispute over the role of the Jewish Socialist Bund within the framework of the Social Democratic Party. The Bund had played an important part in organizing the oppressed Jews in Poland and Russia. Established along democratic lines, it contained some of the most effective political leaders in Russia. The officials of the Bund insisted on having complete autonomy in dealing with Jewish problems. Such a role, however, conflicted sharply with Lenin's concept of a highly centralized revolutionary party. Under his plan all groups would be required to follow the policies and decisions of a small band of top leaders. He argued that to give autonomy to the Bund would lead to similar demands from other member organizations. Thus it would undermine the principle of centralized leadership which he had set forth so painstakingly in *What's to Be Done?*

Surprisingly, George Plekhanov lined up in full support of Lenin! Not so Jules Martov, Paul Axelrod and Leon Trotsky. They agreed on the need for a centralized party and opposed the demands of the Jewish Bund for complete autonomy. But they also felt that Lenin wanted to go too far. They vigorously rejected his notion of an elite party that would seize power "in the name of the proletariat." Martov took the floor to advocate a "broad party" rather than a select party of professional revolutionaries whose members "abdicated their right to think." He pleaded for a party that would be open to any worker or intellectual who believed in its program. And he demanded, furthermore, that party membership carry with it the right to a voice in the party's affairs.

Trotsky got up and sided with Martov. Lenin was shocked and angered. Trotsky reminded the delegates that Marx's *Communist Manifesto* called for majority action in order to achieve the dictatorship of the working class. Paraphrasing Marx, Trotsky declared:

> The rule of the working class was inconceivable until the great mass of them were united in desiring it. Then they would be an overwhelming majority. This would not be the dictatorship of a little band of conspirators or a minority party, but of the immense majority in the interests of the immense majority, to prevent counter-revolution. In short, it would represent the victory of true democracy.

Many delegates went even further than Trotsky and opposed the concept of a "dictatorship of the working class" altogether. Why replace one dictatorship—the tsarist dictatorship—with another? they argued angrily. How could the party talk about freedom of speech, assembly, press and other rights when the existence of a revolutionary dictatorship of the proletariat would automatically nullify these rights?

In the midst of the debate the Congress was interrupted by a sudden directive from the Belgian police banning the meeting on Belgian soil. Hastily, plans were made to adjourn and resume the Congress in London. The delegates proceeded by train and boat to England, where the arguments continued.

In spite of the opposition of Martov, Trotsky and others, it became pointedly clear that Lenin's call for a centralized dictatorial party was making headway. The disgusted representatives of the Jewish Bund got up and walked out of the Congress. Although dismayed by the loss of one of the party's most important groups, the delegates continued to line up in favor of Lenin's program.

Sensing victory, Lenin insisted that every detail of his plan be accepted exactly as he had outlined it. He brooked no compromise or opposition. He attacked the "chicaneries and idiocies" of his opponents and denounced them in bitter personal attacks. Jules Martov, a gentle person who had been close to him earlier, was astonished by Lenin's rude, domineering behavior, which struck him as that of a madman.

Actually Lenin was under considerable strain. He ate little and was getting almost no sleep. Physical and mental fatigue had brought him to the point of nervous exhaustion. Brusque and sharp-tongued even with his supporters, he alienated almost everyone with whom he had contact.

Aided by Plekhanov's support as well as the departure of the Jewish Bund delegates who were opposed to his plan, Lenin won by a narrow margin. Flushed with victory, he immediately designated his supporters as the *Bolsheviki*—or "majority." Those who had voted against him he referred to as the *Mensheviki*—or "minority." It was a shrewd move which he sensed would have great propaganda value in the future. Even if he should lose majority backing, the name *Bolsheviki* would stick, thus implying that his side really spoke for most of the Social Democrats.

Lenin now set to work to regain control of the *Iskra* board. Of the six editors, only he and Plekhanov were Bolsheviks. All the others had voted with the Menshevik position. Lenin got the Congress to pass a resolution calling for the reduction of the *Iskra* board to three members—Plekhanov, Martov and himself. Axelrod, Potresov and Vera Zasulich were deeply hurt at being ousted, but they could do nothing about it.

Lenin's strategy in keeping Martov on the board was calculated to give the impression he wanted to work with the Mensheviks in the interest of party harmony. At the same time, he knew that Martov would be powerless since he would be outnumbered by himself and Plekhanov.

However, events of the following weeks indicated that Lenin had outreached himself. While Plekhanov had supported him at the Congress in calling for a strong, centralized party, he had no intention of becoming Lenin's rubber stamp. Nor did he intend to turn his back on his old comrades—Axelrod, Potresov and Vera Zasulich—even though they had differed with him.

Lenin lost support outside of *Iskra,* too. His tyrannical behavior in Brussels and London had alienated many Bolsheviks as well as Mensheviks. Some former associates such as Leon Trotsky now considered him "a despot and terrorist."

To Lenin it seemed that his victory at the Congress had turned to ashes overnight. Instead of strengthening his grip on the party, his personal support was melting away. Plekhanov, supported by Martov, invited Axelrod, Potresov and Vera Zasulich to rejoin *Iskra.* Thus the tables were turned on Lenin.

He was now as completely and utterly alone as he had been before the Congress. Faced with the prospect of being outvoted at every turn, Lenin made a critical decision. He would leave *Iskra!* Better to quit than undergo the humiliation of powerlessness and defeat. In November 1903, less than four months after the Congress, a disillusioned and heartsick Lenin submitted his resignation. It was tantamount to severing relations with the party itself.

Nevertheless Lenin had no intention of abandoning revolutionary politics. He still had a few personal followers in Geneva. More important, he had retained excellent contacts with the secret party agents in Russia, developed while he controlled the *Iskra* circulation lists. Now he decided to put them to good use. He sent out letters asking for funds to publish a new newspaper to be known as *Vperyod*—or "Forward." It would be a truly revolutionary paper—not like *Iskra*, which he asserted had become a tool of "the so-called ambassadors of the working class, Plekhanov, Martov and the rest."

While Lenin waited for the campaign to bring results, he promised Nadezhda that he would take a vacation from politics. In the summer of 1904 they were joined by a friend, an attractive young revolutionary named Maria Essen, on a hiking tour of the Swiss mountains. It was a rejuvenating experience, one that reminded Lenin of his boyhood days in the hills near the Volga. Wandering the countryside with rucksacks on their backs, they visited magnificent old castles and drank in the majestic beauty of the craggy peaks.

But forgetting politics was easier said than done. At one point the small party made its way to the summit of a particularly inviting mountain. The climb became steeper and more arduous as they neared the top. While Nadezhda and Maria struggled to keep up, Lenin strode briskly ahead in the knee-deep snow. When they came to the peak, the two women gazed breathlessly down on a landscape stretching in all directions in marvelous colors. Beneath them, far below the sea of white snow, were rich green Alpine pastures alive with flowers of every conceivable hue. But Lenin was unaware of the magnificent scenery. Sitting off to one side, he was absorbed in his own thoughts. Suddenly he exclaimed, "All the same, those Mensheviks—they're all wrong!"

By fall, money started coming in for the new newspaper. However the contributions arrived in trickles rather than the flood Lenin had expected. Although he and Nadezhda were living from hand to mouth, he supplemented the *Vperyod* fund by adding small sums he earned by lecturing. As the new year approached, he was still far from the two thousand rubles a month which he estimated he needed to begin publishing. Nevertheless, he decided to launch the paper anyway, even if it meant going into debt.

It was not merely impatience that drove Lenin to speed up the publication of *Vperyod*. He had received visits from persons just arrived from Russia who confirmed what the speakers at the Congress had indicated. The country *was* suffering from mass unrest. Discontent was especially high now because the country found itself in a war with Japan that was highly unpopular. Economically it was hurting the nation and diverting the government's attention from needed domestic reforms.

The Russo-Japanese War had begun the previous year. Russia had recently occupied Manchuria and had leased Port Arthur from China, moves that conflicted with Japan's own ambitions in eastern Asia. In February 1904, a well-organized, disciplined and modernly equipped Japanese army opened hostilities. Thereafter Japan quickly won a series of impressive victories against Russian forces whose main line of supply was the three-thousand-mile-long single-track Trans-Siberian Railway.

Discontent within Russia grew as the disorganization and inefficiency of the mammoth Russian army became apparent. In addition, millions of Russians could not understand why Russia was fighting Japan at all. In July, the Russian Far Eastern Fleet was completely destroyed as it attempted to leave the shelter of Port Arthur and Vladivostok.

Such reports of heavy losses in a war that did not have popular support continued to provoke domestic strife. Radical groups voiced loud opposition to the government's policies. Terrorism increased. Within a single month, the Governor-General of Finland and Russia's Minister of the Interior were assassinated. The Russian political vat was beginning to boil over.

In Geneva, Lenin was well aware of the troubles brewing in Russia. He knew that the sooner he got out *Vperyod,* the quicker he could begin exploiting public discontent in Russia. He saw in such a situation great potential for forming a new political movement. In preparing copy for the first issue of the newspaper, which was to come out in January 1905, Lenin wrote:

> A military collapse is now inevitable, and together with it there will come inevitably a tenfold increase of unrest, discontent and rebellion. For that moment we must prepare with all energy. At that moment one of those outbreaks which are occurring, now here, now there, with such growing frequency, will develop into

a tremendous popular movement. At that moment the proletariat will rise to take its place at the head of the insurrection to win freedom for the entire people and to secure for the working classes the possibility of waging an open and broad struggle for socialism, a struggle enriched by the whole experience of Europe.

Events moved ahead even more swiftly than Lenin had dared hope. Less than three weeks after the first issue of *Vperyod*, blood stained the streets of St. Petersburg.

It happened on Sunday morning, January 22, 1905. On that day Father George Gapon, a Russian Orthodox priest, led a procession of two hundred thousand men, women and children through the snow-blanketed capital. Their destination was the Tsar's Winter Palace where they hoped to present a petition to Nicholas II. The crowd was orderly and good-tempered, even humble. They carried ikons and banners with large painted portraits of the Tsar, and as they marched along they solemnly sang "God Save the Tsar." Everybody fully expected Nicholas to appear at a window of the Winter Palace, deliver a short speech and give them his blessing.

The huge procession had its origin in an unusual labor movement born several years earlier. Technically, unions were still illegal in Russia. In 1901, following the great industrial strikes of the 1890's, several of the Tsar's advisers came up with a crafty plan. Since there was no way to stop the growth of illegal unionism, why not use it to the government's advantage? The idea was simple enough. The government would promote the organization of "labor societies" which would appear to perform the functions of unions but in reality would be run by secret police agents. The government would even help finance these "police unions," which would serve as a buffer against radicals and revolutionaries as well as the illegal unions.

The police agents heading the "labor societies" would try to focus the discontent of the membership against business and industry. In this way workers and capitalists would be pitted against each other, thus diverting attention from the government as a target of criticism.

It was a shrewd plan that caught hold immediately. Police unions were established in many of the large industrial cities. Workers by the thousands flocked to join. Intellectuals, radicals and other "troublemakers" were barred from membership. In some cases where workers who joined proved to be hard to handle, they were quietly arrested and deported.

One of the most successful police union organizers was Father George Gapon, a former prison chaplain and son of a Ukrainian peasant. In St. Petersburg, he founded the "Assembly of Russian Factory and Mill Workers," dedicated to the "legal improvement of the conditions of labor and life of the workers." Father Gapon sincerely believed that a union established under the secret direction of the police would help to better the worker's lot. He agreed to work with the police because he was convinced that the government was interested in improving conditions.

The giant march which Father Gapon organized grew out of his conviction that Tsar Nicholas II—Russia's "little father"—affectionately looked upon all his subjects as his children. The priest felt that a peaceful, solemn procession would impress the ruler with the need for better conditions for the people. A respectful petition was drawn up pleading with Nicholas to convene a popularly elected constituent assembly to recommend reforms.

As two hundred thousand people marched quietly through the streets of St. Petersburg on Sunday morning, January 22, they were unaware that Nicholas was not in the capital. Learning of the procession, he had panicked and fled the Winter Palace with his wife and daughters. Instead of their Tsar, Father Gapon's followers found themselves confronted by police and armed troops massed in front of the Winter Palace. The unarmed marchers were ignorant of what was planned for them as they happily neared the palace. Suddenly the soldiers opened fire. Men, women and children began to fall by the hundreds. Cossack troops galloped through the terrified crowd, flailing the marchers with whips. The air was filled with the screams of the injured and dying. Pools of blood crimsoned the white snow for hundreds of yards.

When at last the crowd was dispersed, there were so many bodies lying in the streets of St. Petersburg that they could not be counted.

It was later estimated that as many as five hundred may have been killed and three thousand wounded!

News of the massacre at the Winter Palace swept through Russia like a shock wave. The people bitterly referred to the day as "Bloody Sunday." It was the end of an era. For a decade, the majority of Russians had believed in Nicholas II and in his good intentions. They had given him love and respect, in spite of his vacillating policies and personal shortcomings as a leader. But the rifles that had fired into Father Gapon's procession that morning had blasted away the people's faith in government as well as their reverence for their ruler.

The disappointment and despair of the Russian people were summed up by Father Gapon himself. Having been knocked to the ground during the attack, he had nevertheless managed to escape with his life and flee the country. From abroad he wrote a letter to the Tsar to whom he had given loyalty and devotion that read:

> The innocent blood of workers, their wives and children, lies forever between thee, O soul destroyer, and the Russian people. Moral connection between thee and them may never more be.... Let all the blood which has to be shed, hangman, fall upon thee and thy kindred.

Lenin heard of "Bloody Sunday" the very next day. He and Nadezhda immediately joined other exiles in a Geneva restaurant and sang a revolutionary funeral march for their martyred countrymen.

Lenin was deliriously excited. He was sure that a revolution was starting and wrote to this effect in *Vperyod*. Not long afterward, Father Gapon himself showed up in Geneva. Most of the revolutionary exiles did not trust him because of his suspected former connections with the police. But Lenin met with him and encouraged him to raise funds for weapons to be smuggled to revolutionaries inside Russia. Because of his new-found popularity the priest was able to secure a number of large contributions. With Lenin's help, a load of arms was shipped in a vessel named the

John Grafton. Headed for Russia, the ship ran aground in Finland and blew up. With it went one of Lenin's high hopes of winning a key leadership role in the hoped-for revolution.

In Russia, events rushed ahead without Lenin. Embittered and angry, industrial workers went out on strike by the hundreds of thousands; peasants attacked the manor houses of their landlords, burning, killing and looting. By February, the country was in a crisis state. Already hard-pressed by Japanese victories in the east, the government feared that domestic chaos would lead to complete anarchy.

Meanwhile, a number of exiles made their way back into Russia to fan the flames of revolt. Among them was the young Menshevik Leon Trotsky. Within weeks after "Bloody Sunday" he had managed to smuggle himself into the strife-torn country. He wrote fiery manifestos, established committees, helped organize the striking workers.

By the end of February 1905 the situation was so critical that even the Tsar realized something must be done. He finally agreed to establish an elected National Duma, or legislature. Although it could not pass laws, the Duma would have the power to consult with the Tsar and make recommendations on governmental policy.

Nicholas felt this was a major compromise. Not so the Russian masses. The alienation of the people from their Tsar had gone too far for them to be satisfied with such a concession. By now they were demanding a national constitution, an end to the war with Japan, and universal suffrage.

Furthermore, it was not only the workers who were on the brink of revolt. In the weeks since "Bloody Sunday," they had been joined by the professional classes—teachers, doctors, lawyers, engineers. These groups now formed their own unions and were linked together in a powerful "Union of Unions." Even some members of the armed forces were talking of mutiny!

The unrest continued to spread. In early summer, revolt broke out aboard the *Prince Potemkin,* the most powerful cruiser in Russia's Black Sea fleet. After dumping their officers into the sea, the crew sailed the vessel to Rumania and asked for political refuge.

A mutiny aboard another warship was not nearly as successful. Sixty sailors were shot to death or sent off to prison.

During these tumultuous months, the exiles who remained abroad played almost no part in the march of events. For the past year they had been so busy squabbling among themselves that they were not prepared with a program to take advantage of the "revolution" of 1905.

Perhaps Lenin, as a key figure in the Bolshevik-Menshevik split, felt a sense of guilt at the exiles' helplessness in exploiting a long-awaited opportunity. Perhaps, too, he resented the fact that most of the exiles who had managed to get back to Russia were Mensheviks. He especially chafed at the knowledge that Leon Trotsky was establishing himself as an important leader in the revolution while he, Lenin, was wasting his time in Geneva.

The Russo-Japanese War ended in September 1905. A month earlier, President Theodore Roosevelt of the United States had intervened to bring the two sides to the peace table. He had sent notes to the Tsar and the Mikado—the Emperor of Japan—urging them to negotiate. The invitation was accepted. Each country sent representatives to Portsmouth, New Hampshire, where discussions finally resulted in a peace treaty on September 5. Although both Russia and Japan were to evacuate Manchuria, the terms of the agreement left no doubt that Japan was to be dominant in the Far East. For Russia, it was an embarrassing defeat.

The end of the fighting did little to calm the domestic upheaval in Russia. Although the war had helped to ignite it, the fires of revolt continued to spread.

By early fall of 1905, Lenin could stand it no longer. Convinced that his chance to lead a revolution might be slipping away forever, he decided he must get to Russia immediately.

9.

1905

LENIN'S FAILURE to dash off to Russia at the first sign of trouble was not due to lack of daring or determination, but to miscalculation. He had envisioned himself as the overall strategist of revolution, effecting its course from a distance. To this end he had worked tirelessly, writing fiery editorials for *Vperyod* and engaging in schemes to smuggle weapons into Russia. The meetings of his small band of followers were devoted to the study of guerrilla techniques, sabotage and street fighting.

Unfortunately for Lenin, events in Russia were so tumultuous that no absentee revolutionary a thousand miles from the scene could hope to influence their direction. The knowledge that few were listening to him was a bitter pill to swallow. It was this realization that finally convinced him he must get to Russia at all costs.

In October, Lenin left Nadezhda in Geneva and made his way to Stockholm by train. A fellow revolutionary was supposed to give him a false passport, but the man never showed up. In desperation Lenin telephoned or telegraphed every contact he could think of in western Europe. It cost him two weeks of delay, but finally he succeeded in getting his credentials. Even with the papers his troubles were not over. The steamer that was to carry him to Russia was delayed by storms.

When he finally reached St. Petersburg, his frustration mounted. Russia was in the throes of revolution, but he felt he was already too late. The leadership was firmly in the hands of Mensheviks and labor leaders; there was little he could do to seize the reins.

The nation was experiencing a paralyzing general strike. The government was in danger of being brought to its knees. *Soviets*—the Russian word for "councils"—of Workers' Delegates had sprung up in St. Petersburg and Moscow. Established to organize and direct the strike, the soviets were the real representatives of the organized power of the working class and spoke for the workers.

By the time Lenin arrived in Russia, Trotsky, using a false passport and calling himself "Yanovsky," had risen to the chairmanship of the St. Petersburg Soviet. It was an eminent position for a young revolutionary still in his twenties.

Lenin was confused and dismayed. The very existence of the soviets seemed to contradict his own cherished blueprint for revolution. The workers' councils represented the masses. They were not elite leadership cadres. Thus, they violated every principal of revolution he had laid down in *What's to Be Done?* He acknowledged to others that Trotsky had earned his eminence by his "tireless and striking work." Nevertheless, he was resentful because the Mensheviks were in control and there was nothing he could do about it. He did not participate in the meetings of the St. Petersburg Soviet, nor was he invited to do so. Indeed, in almost every respect, he felt like an outsider in the capital. Furthermore, from the moment he entered Russia, his trail had been picked up by the secret police. Though they did not arrest him, he was aware of their presence. So he had to be on his guard every moment to avoid an indiscretion that might betray one of his revolutionary contacts.

The pressure on the Tsar to go along with the demand for reforms was greater than ever. In addition to the general strike, many returning soldiers began to riot. Frustrated by their defeat at the hands of Japan, they blamed government incompetence and demanded change. In several units, officers were shot and the troops went out into the streets to join the strikers.

On October 30, the Tsar finally gave in. The capitulation was inevitable. By now Russia was threatened with economic collapse as well as anarchy. Nicholas agreed to some of the same reforms that Father Gapon had requested ten months earlier. He issued what came to be known as the October Manifesto. In it he promised the people the rights of habeas corpus, freedom of speech and assembly, and a new constitution. The Tsar gave a vague pledge that the principle of universal suffrage would be established. Moreover, he agreed that no law would be passed without the consent of the elected Duma, the legislature which he had announced the previous February.

Most of the strikers eagerly accepted the Manifesto. Leon Trotsky, speaking for the St. Petersburg Soviet, denounced it as a hoax. He argued that while it seemed to give everything, it actually gave nothing:

> Freedom of assembly is granted but the assemblies are surrounded by the military. Freedom of speech is granted but the censorship exists even as before. Freedom of knowledge is granted but the universities are occupied by troops. Inviolability of person is granted but the prisons are overflowing.

In spite of Trotsky's vigorous opposition to the Manifesto, he failed to obtain the support he needed. The workers were simply too hungry and too tired to continue the strike. Prices had risen, food was scarce, wages had stopped. The strikers convinced themselves they had won the freedoms they had sought. By the third of November, the strike was over and the workers went back to their jobs. But the truce proved to be short-lived.

The agitation of the workers and radicals had given rise to an ugly counterrevolutionary force. Throughout Russia hoodlum elements, religious fanatics and the ignorant and frustrated formed terrorist bands to stamp out the anti-Tsarist forces. Known as the "Black Hundreds," these groups operated with the approval, sometimes even with the help, of the police. Carrying pictures of Nicholas II and singing "God Save the Tsar," they committed outrageous acts of pillage, assault and murder in the name of superpatriotism.

Seeking scapegoats, the "Black Hundreds" blamed Russia's defeat by Japan as well as all her domestic woes on "Poles and Jews."

Vicious pogroms were organized against these minority groups. In addition, working-class neighborhoods were invaded and many homes were looted and burned.

The workers responded by arming themselves. They formed defense companies and distributed rifles, pistols, daggers, pikes and brass knuckles. St. Petersburg and Moscow were soon transformed into armed camps.

Nevertheless, the police, aided by the terrorism of the "Black Hundreds," began to regain the control they had lost during the strike. Ignoring the provisions of the October Manifesto, the government soon sent troops into the provinces to punish the peasants. Those who had been leaders in the antigovernment activity were lined up and shot without trial. Other participants were flogged and their huts burned. In the larger cities the police moved in and arrested many of the former strike leaders.

The members of the St. Petersburg Soviet now saw that Trotsky had been right. The Tsar *had* betrayed them. The actions of the police made it clear that Nicholas had no intention of implementing the October Manifesto. The soviet quickly voted a second general strike for the middle of November. But because events were happening so fast there was no time to organize it properly. For example, there was little opportunity to win the support of other groups such as the shopkeepers and government employees who had supported the earlier strike. As a result, the effort was limited almost solely to the factory workers. It proved ineffectual and had to be called off after three days.

Early in December, the police arrested the entire leadership of the St. Petersburg Soviet, including Chairman Trotsky, who was still going under the name of Yanovsky. The remaining members declared a new general strike. As the strike spread to other cities, including Moscow, Russia was again plunged into nationwide turmoil.

Lenin, out of things until now, proceeded from St. Petersburg to Moscow, where the strike was having a devastating effect. There he soon found an outlet for his leadership ambitions. Unlike the St. Petersburg Soviet, where the Mensheviks were in control, the Moscow leadership was lodged in a federated soviet of united

Bolsheviks and Mensheviks. As acknowledged leader of the Bolshevik faction, Lenin quickly gained an important voice.

On December 26, in the middle of the strike, he left Moscow to slip over the border into Finland to attend a Bolshevik conference. As soon as he left, Moscow was plunged into full-scale warfare.

The Moscow strike had started peacefully enough. The workers were in good humor, and there seemed little likelihood of violence. However, as the days passed there were occasional instances of sniping against the police. Shots were returned and the mood of the police and the strikers grew uglier. Government troops armed with heavy artillery and machine guns were shipped into Moscow. Barricades were erected in the streets. By this time workers, operating in guerrilla companies of twos and threes, were making hit-and-run attacks on the police and troops. They struck quickly from doorways, windows and rooftops, then melted away into the jungle of Moscow's working-class districts.

As the fighting reached its peak, the government troops numbered more than ten thousand fully armed men. The workers had a total of two hundred pistols and a few hunting rifles. They realized almost from the start that they were no match for the troops. Besides their lack of weapons they had no real plan of action. Yet they retained a desperate hope that at least some of the troops would mutiny and join them.

It did not happen. There was no mass mutiny of soldiers. The army managed to clear the center of the city and confine the guerrillas to the Presnaya district where working-class families lived. For the next three days long-range artillery was used to bombard the area indiscriminately. Factories and houses were destroyed; hundreds of men, women and children were killed or wounded. Nevertheless, the workers managed to hold out for almost a week!

By New Year's Day it was all over. As the police and troops entered the Presnaya, they wreaked savage vengeance. Most of the able-bodied armed fighters had managed to escape. When an occasional guerrilla was seized, he was put to death immediately. The ones who were left were mostly women, children and the wounded. Many were beaten and assaulted by the soldiers. Thousands were thrown into jail. Some of the wounded were dragged from ambulances and murdered in cold blood.

The workers had revolted—and lost. The year 1905 had begun with the "Bloody Sunday" massacre of Father Gapon's followers. It had ended with the death of an estimated thousand more Russians and the total devastation of a quarter of the city of Moscow. The people of Russia had paid dearly for their lost revolution.

Lenin returned to Moscow from Finland in the middle of January. He found the city still in the throes of shock. There was a sinister calm in the air. The signs of death and destruction were everywhere. It was not at all the way he had imagined a revolution would be. In the final analysis it had been an ill-prepared spontaneous uprising, without plan, discipline or goal. Thus it had violated all the principles he himself had set down as being necessary for a successful revolution.

The Tsar called the first meeting of the Duma, which he had promised the previous year, for March 1906. Lenin spent the weeks after his return denouncing the Duma to anyone who would listen. The Duma was a farce, he warned. It would have no real power and should be boycotted by all workers and revolutionaries. Yet few listened. For the disillusioned workers who had gambled and lost, the Duma was at least a tiny crumb of achievement.

In preparation for the Duma elections, the Tsar legalized Russia's political parties. There was vigorous campaigning among all the groups except the Bolsheviks. The elections were to be indirect. The Russian people would vote for electors, who in turn would choose the delegates to the Duma. It was an unwieldy, unsatisfactory procedure, but Nicholas refused to provide an alternative.

Within weeks after the newly elected Duma members took their seats, there was even more widespread frustration than before. The Duma had been given the trappings of a democratic legislature but it had no real power. Petition after petition was passed by the assembly, without effect. The Duma called for the release of political prisoners, universal voting rights and direct elections. All were rejected by the Tsar.

Nicholas himself felt a renewed sense of power. Having broken the back of the revolution, he knew he was in control again. Moreover, he felt it useful to demonstrate this fact to the people. Therefore when the Duma called for reforms that would provide more land for the peasants, the Tsar decided to do more than merely exercise his veto. Fearful that such a recommendation would stir up the peasants again, he decided to disband the Duma altogether. Troops were sent to surround the palace where the legislature was meeting. The delegates were ordered to adjourn. They did.

The disillusionment of the Russian people was complete.

For the next year and a half Lenin remained in Russia. He shuttled back and forth between Finland, St. Petersburg and Moscow. He wrote anonymous tracts, as well as articles for *Vperyod*, urging preparations for a new revolution. But the workers were physically and psychologically exhausted. Overcome by a sense of hopelessness and helplessness, they were in no mood to launch a new revolution.

In the spring of 1907 the Social Democratic Party held its Fifth Congress, in London. Lenin traveled from Moscow to attend the meeting. Its purpose was to heal the breach between the Mensheviks and Bolsheviks and reunite the party. But the split was too wide to be healed. Lenin raged against the Mensheviks and liberals and engaged in a nasty personal exchange with Leon Trotsky. Trotsky had been exiled to Siberia following his arrest in St. Petersburg but had managed to escape by persuading a peasant to carry him more than four hundred miles by sleigh.

Among Lenin's new supporters at the London Conference was a swarthy, pock-marked young man from Georgia, a southern province of Russia. His name was Joseph Djugashvili. As a boy he had been nicknamed Soso. But in later years he would become better known as Joseph Stalin.

In November 1907, Lenin left Russia to return to Switzerland. Geneva seemed cold, cheerless and remote. Nadezhda's mother lived with them. A little later they were joined by Lenin's younger sister, Maria. Lenin wrote constantly, railing against the Mensheviks and other rival factions.

At night there was little to do but go to the cinema or theater. During the two years he had been in Russia most of his followers in Geneva had departed, so that now he felt quite alone. However, there were occasional holidays when he and Nadezhda would visit friends in other countries. Maxim Gorky, the famous Russian novelist, lived at Capri, Italy, and he and Lenin became friendly. Gorky had founded a "retreat" at Capri for Russian revolutionary exiles. Lenin visited the resort.

Later Gorky described Lenin as two people. On the one hand, he was a friendly, good-natured guest who loved fishing and swimming and chatted amiably with the native Italians on Capri. On other occasions, he was the ruthless, inflexible Bolshevik who argued bitterly with his fellow revolutionaries and showed utter contempt for "Mensheviks and liberals." The heated debates with the other Russian guests grew so unpleasant that they did not hide the fact that Lenin's continued presence was unwelcome. As a result, he left Capri after only a few days, although he remained on good terms with Gorky.

By the fall of 1908, Lenin found the atmosphere in Geneva so cold and uninteresting that he knew he must leave. Almost on impulse he, Nadezhda, Nadezhda's mother and his sister Maria packed up their things and moved to Paris.

Meanwhile, the Tsar continued to reconsolidate his power in Russia. As usual, however, Nicholas' policies were often inconsistent and occasionally contradictory. While the revolution of 1905 had failed, it had succeeded in liberating within the government itself pressure for a policy of moderation. For example, although Nicholas had disbanded the first Duma, his more liberal ministers persuaded him not to drop the Duma concept altogether. They argued that the Russian people must be given a political outlet if the pressures for another revolt were to be kept under control. Nicholas gave in. Additional Dumas were convened. But the Tsar was steadfast in his refusal to grant the legislatures real power.

Among the most brilliant of Nicholas' moderate ministers was Count Sergei Witte, Russia's greatest industrializer and financier. For a decade Count Witte had helped Russia reform her backward economy by securing foreign loans and credits. He was considered the father of Russian industrialization, having spurred the development of new railroads and factories at a phenomenal rate. A constitutional liberal, he warned the Tsar that real political reform must be introduced in order to provide the internal stability Russia needed for continued economic growth.

Advisers such as Count Witte encountered the active opposition of old-guard ministers who demanded that the nation return to the past. They counseled the Tsar to reject every suggestion that the people be given a greater voice in government. The weak and vacillating Nicholas found it hard to decide which course to follow. His policies, therefore, were a curious combination of reactionary autocratic measures tempered by occasional ventures in the direction of moderation.

In the end, however, reaction triumphed. A key factor was the malevolent influence of a sinister "holy man" named Gregory Rasputin. The son of a Siberian peasant, Rasputin was a ne'er-do-well who had been arrested for thievery and drunkenness in his youth. In his thirties, he joined a strange religious sect which preached salvation through sin and repentance.

Uncouth in appearance and coarse in manner, Rasputin had nevertheless gained a reputation as a faith healer—one who could produce "miracle cures." In the early 1900's he made his way to St. Petersburg, where he soon became a favorite among wealthy court women. Eventually, he came to the attention of the Tsar and the Empress.

Nicholas was married to Alexandra Fyodorovna, a granddaughter of Queen Victoria. Born Alice, Princess of Hesse-Darmstadt, the Empress was affectionately known to her family as Alix. The handsome, strong-willed woman gave birth to four daughters, although she and the Tsar had been praying for a son to inherit the throne. Finally, in 1904, Alix had a son. The tiny prince, known as the Tsarevitch, was named Alexis.

Prince Alexis was found to be suffering from hemophilia, the dreaded bleeding disease. Any slight accident, even a mild bump, could set off a fatal hemorrhage. The distraught royal couple searched desperately for help. But the doctors were powerless, for there was no known cure for hemophilia.

A lady in waiting, the Grand Duchess Militsa, urged the Empress to call in Gregory Rasputin. The frantic Alix, ready to try anything, promised to keep the advice in mind. One day while

Alexis was having a bleeding spell, Nicholas, at his wife's insistence, summoned the "monk" who was supposed to work miracles.

Rasputin was brought to the bedroom of the Tsarevitch. Taking a seat beside the little boy, he began to talk in a low, soothing voice. He told stories, sang peasant songs and made strange, mystical signs with his hands. After a long time, he got up, turned to the royal couple and informed them that the bleeding had stopped!

The Tsar and the Empress could scarcely believe what they themselves had seen. The royal physicians were called in to examine Alexis. They confirmed that the bleeding had been brought under control. It was almost beyond comprehension. Rasputin had done what the most knowledgeable physicians in Europe had been unable to do.

The doctors understandably viewed the black-garbed faith healer with distaste mingled with envy. They suspected he had tried hypnosis on the little boy. In fact, mesmerism was a technique used by some physicians down through the generations to deaden pain and to treat certain forms of mental illness. But in spite of their distrust of this self-proclaimed holy man, the doctors could not deny that his method had worked. When additional attacks occurred, Rasputin was again summoned to use his mysterious healing power. Each time he succeeded in stopping the bleeding.

Alix and the Tsar were so impressed that overnight Rasputin became an important figure in the court. Slowly but surely he gained influence over the Empress and, through her, over the Tsar himself. At first he used his power mainly in church appointments. But as time went on he was to exert an influence over political affairs as well. He had friends named to important posts without regard to their qualifications. And he began to meddle in state policy to such an extent that many areas of government were reduced to chaos. As the years passed, the heavy hand of an ignorant and reactionary peasant-turned-holy-man was felt more and more throughout the empire.

From his refuge in Paris, Lenin observed developments in Russia with the detached objectivity of the professional revolutionary. The more reactionary the Tsar's government became and the more Russia bled, the more certain he was that his own moment in history would come.

10.

Storm Over Europe

IN PARIS, the Lenins lived in a nicely furnished apartment at 24 Rue Beaunier, a pleasant residential street. It was a far cry from their shabby working-class quarters in Geneva. Although the political influence of the Social Democrats had been ebbing since the failure of the 1905 uprising, their financial outlook had improved. The party had received a number of substantial contributions, including a legacy of more than a quarter of a million francs from a wealthy revolutionary sympathizer.

Lenin and the Bolsheviks managed to gain control of the fund, known as the Schmitt legacy, through complex legal maneuvers. Part of the money was used to support full-time revolutionaries such as Lenin himself.

Secret funds were also available to the Bolshevik faction from illegal sources. Throughout Russia the most militant Bolsheviks had established "expropriation" committees, which were really outlaw bands engaged in armed robbery of banks, post offices and trains. The proceeds were to be used to finance the socialist revolution. One of the most desperate and successful of these gangs roamed the Caucasus Mountains in southern Russia. It was headed by the young Georgian Bolshevik Joseph Djugashvili.

A series of bank robberies and murders netted millions of rubles. But they also brought notoriety which dismayed the Mensheviks.

It was feared that the banditry would alienate supporters of the Social Democratic Party. The moderates also objected to the use of "dirty money" on ethical grounds.

Lenin had no such moralistic compunctions. Since he believed the ends justified any means necessary to achieve them, he felt "expropriation" was a sound revolutionary technique. The question of bad publicity did not concern him. At this juncture he wanted to build a small, disciplined revolutionary cadre, not impress the masses. He saw in the robberies a practical way to finance the Bolshevik effort. The Mensheviks repeatedly denounced Lenin and his followers for permitting outlaw practices, but the criticism was coolly ignored.

Life in Paris was calm. Lenin worked in the library and attended conferences and meetings with other political exiles living there. He also completed the manuscript of a new book entitled *Materialism and Empirio-Criticism*. It was a strident attack on those who did not agree with the Leninist interpretation of Marxist doctrine.

Lenin loved Paris. He frequently railed at the inefficiency and red tape of the French. Yet he considered Paris the most beautiful of all cities. He loved the crowded streets, the outdoor cafés, the buzz of human activity that seemed to pervade all of Paris. Like many other Parisians, Lenin and his family vacationed in the south of France on the shores of the placid, blue Mediterranean.

The Lenins did not do much entertaining. But when they did have a guest it was Lenin himself who usually cleaned up after dinner. Although the house was filled with women, he enjoyed such tasks as washing the dishes. He actually considered it a form of relaxation. First-time visitors were often astounded, if not amused, by the sight of the famous Bolshevik leader lecturing on revolutionary techniques while scrubbing a pot over the kitchen sink.

In 1910, Lenin's interests took a new turn. As a husband he had earned a reputation as a model of puritanical existence. Except for his wife, there had been no serious romantic attachments in his life. Everybody considered his and Nadezhda's marriage idyllic.

One day, Lenin was introduced to Elisabeth Armand, an attractive Bolshevik. She was known in the party as Inessa. Born in France, she had been married to a wealthy Moscow manufacturer and had given birth to five children. Then she had become obsessed by revolutionary politics and left her husband to work for the Bolsheviks, taking two of her children with her.

Lenin was immediately attracted to the youthful-looking Inessa. At thirty, she seemed ten years younger. Moreover she was charming, vivacious and intelligent, reminding him in many ways of his own dead sister, Olga. They were often seen together taking long walks in the park or conversing animatedly at a sidewalk café. Soon the entire Russian exile community in Paris was rife with rumor and speculation.

Nadezhda met Inessa and liked her. She knew her husband was seeing a great deal of the young woman but assumed they were involved in party business. In time, she came to realize Vladimir's interest in Inessa was romantic as well as political. She offered to leave him so he could marry the attractive Bolshevik. But Lenin would not dream of divorcing Nadezhda, for whom he still had a deep affection. He considered her a necessary part of his existence. Indeed, he was very much a creature of habit and depended on her for the orderly running of his affairs. The prospect of a major upheaval in his personal life frightened him. Thus, he insisted that they continue as husband and wife. At the same time he and Inessa remained very close friends, a relationship that did not seem to offend Nadezhda at all.

The months passed with life going on pretty much as before. There were the usual squabbles with the Mensheviks, endless party conferences and the publication of new newspapers or magazines, which survived for a year or so, then died. In 1911 Lenin decided to start a "school" to train underground workers. The idea came from Maxim Gorky's retreat for exiles on Capri. Lenin established his school in the village of Longjumeau on the outskirts of Paris and invited apprentice revolutionaries to enroll without charge.

As a schoolmaster he was masterful. He prepared his lectures with great care. The subjects included agrarianism, political economy and the practice of socialism. He invited other Bolshevik leaders to discuss such subjects as the history of the Social Democratic Party, socialist literature and foreign socialist movements. Nadezhda and Inessa Armand assisted in the administration of the school.

The student body had several enrollees who later were revealed as Russian police spies. A few established such close ties with Lenin that they were able to report almost every detail of Bolshevik activity to their superiors. Lenin, whose judgment of people was often faulty, tended to discount stories of police infiltration. When indications of such activity were brought to his attention, he usually pooh-poohed them as baseless.

One of the most notorious of the police spies was a man named Roman Malinovsky. He ingratiated himself with Lenin and became one of his intimates. Although rumors circulated through the party of Malinovsky's police connections, Lenin brushed them off as the spiteful inventions of his Menshevik enemies.

By 1912 the Bolsheviks and Mensheviks had acquired legal standing in Russia as separate factions of the Social Democratic Party. This meant that each could nominate candidates to stand for election to the Duma. Originally, Lenin and the Bolsheviks had denounced the Duma and had urged everybody to boycott it because the Tsar had refused to grant it real power. The Mensheviks had argued against a boycott. By now Lenin realized that the Mensheviks had been right—that his earlier stand had been a tactical blunder. Even if the Duma had no real power, it could serve as an effective platform for selling a revolutionary program to the Russian people. Accordingly, the Bolsheviks set out to get as many of their candidates as possible elected. They founded a legal daily newspaper named *Pravda* as a propaganda organ. The Mensheviks established a daily called *Luch*.

The Bolsheviks succeeded in obtaining six Duma seats. The Mensheviks elected seven deputies. In order to exert maximum influence, the Bolshevik and Menshevik delegates, supported by their newspapers, agreed to form a single Duma Fraction. When Lenin learned of the unification movement, he was furious. He wrote articles for *Pravda* fuming against reconciliation with the Mensheviks. Many of his vitriolic statements were edited out of the manuscripts before they saw print. He wrote irate letters to the editorial board in St. Petersburg, but they were ignored.

Among the Bolsheviks elected to the Duma was Roman Malinovsky, the secret police spy who had become Lenin's intimate! Malinovsky, acting on orders from the police, strongly opposed unification. Lenin, of course, was still ignorant of Malinovsky's police connections and continued to shrug off rumors that he might be a spy. He knew only that Malinovsky was following "true" Bolshevik principles in opposing unity. Consequently, he urged the delegate to use every pretext he could devise to lead the Bolshevik Duma group to an open break with the Mensheviks. Thus, Lenin was unknowingly allying himself with the secret police in encouraging a disruption of the united fraction!

Malinovsky attacked the Menshevik delegates as "false proletarians." He pointed out that none of them had ever worked in an industrial job. How could they, then, adequately represent the laboring masses? he demanded to know.

Meanwhile, Lenin set about to win control of *Pravda*. He secretly sent Bolshevik agents loyal to himself to St. Petersburg to force a change in the paper's editorial policy. They were Jacob Sverdlov and Lev Kamenev, two of his best organizers, and Joseph Djugashvili, the Georgian "expropriator." Since all were wanted by the police, only Malinovsky was told of their real identities. They agitated so effectively that they soon convinced the *Pravda* board that Lenin spoke for the Bolshevik majority. Early in 1913, Lenin was able to write to Sverdlov: "Today we learned about the beginning of reforms on *Pravda*. A thousand greetings, congratulations and good wishes . . ."

With the hostile editorial board brought into line, the newspaper declared war on the Mensheviks. Conciliation with "Menshevik tendencies" was denounced daily in its pages. The pace of the attack was stepped up with the appointment of a new editor-in-chief named Miron Chernomazov. The new editor was such an ardent supporter of the Leninist anti-unity line that Lenin himself could not have made a stronger case. Later Chernomazov, too, was to be unmasked as a paid police agent.

Overnight, the spirit of togetherness vanished from the united Duma Fraction. Personal attacks and charges of treason against the working class were traded. The breach grew wider. By the spring of 1913 the break between the Bolsheviks and Mensheviks was complete and permanent.

Lenin was overjoyed. His strategy had worked out even more successfully than he could have imagined. However, his sense of triumph was tempered by the sobering news that Sverdlov and Djugashvili had been arrested and sent to Siberia. Kamenev just managed to escape the police net. It never occurred to Lenin to suspect Malinovsky, who alone knew of the Bolshevik agents' identities while they were in St. Petersburg.

In the following weeks and months dozens of other arrests were made. Not so curiously, in almost every instance those arrested had had some contact with Roman Malinovsky just a short time before.

In spite of Lenin's stubborn refusal to entertain accusations against the Bolshevik Duma delegate, other party members grew more suspicious of him by the day. The rumors finally got back to Malinovsky himself. On May 8, 1914, he unexpectedly handed in his resignation as a member of the Duma "for reasons of health" and mysteriously left Russia.

Consternation and amazement abounded in political circles. The Bolsheviks were embarrassed and dismayed as the story of Malinovsky's police connections leaked out in some detail. Lenin, who was particularly shocked and embittered, wrote to a friend: "We are going out of our minds with this idiocy." When suspicions were raised about Miron Chernomazov, the editor-in-chief of *Pravda*, he was quietly removed from the paper. This time Lenin did not dismiss the rumors as the invention of the Mensheviks.

Fortunately for the Bolsheviks, they were spared further embarrassment over the Malinovsky affair. Larger events were looming that would soon cause the world to forget everything else. By the summer of 1914, war was already darkening the horizon.

For years, central Europe had been a cauldron of nationalistic ambitions and international rivalries. The small Balkan states were the pawns in a competition between the great powers. Both the Austro-Hungarian Empire of Franz Joseph and the Russian Empire of Tsar Nicholas II had been casting covetous eyes on the Balkans.

Relations between the two sides worsened. As tensions increased, there was growing talk of war.

On June 28, 1914, on the crowded streets of Sarajevo, capital of Bosnia, a Serbian youth named Gavril Princip assassinated Archduke Francis Ferdinand, heir to the Austro-Hungarian throne. It was the fuse that was to set off World War I. Within six weeks, the powder keg exploded and all Europe was aflame.

The war caught Lenin and the other revolutionaries by surprise. He had thought about war and discussed it often. But like many others, he was convinced a major war over the Balkans was such madness it would never come to pass. True, as a Bolshevik, he considered a capitalist war ideal for his revolutionary purposes. But he assured Nadezhda, Inessa Armand and others that it would never take place.

"A war between Austria and Russia would be a very useful thing for the revolution in all of eastern Europe," he noted to a friend. "Yet it is not likely that Franz Joseph and Nikolasha [Tsar Nicholas II] will give us that pleasure."

Indeed, the war took Lenin so unawares that when it did break out he was in Austria, working on party business under his legal name. As an enemy alien, he was immediately thrown into prison. However, he was released after twelve days when an Austrian socialist deputy convinced his government that the prisoner Vladimir Ulyanov was actually an enemy of the tsarist government.

The Lenins immediately resettled in neutral Switzerland. This time he and Nadezhda chose Berne, because the cost of living was lower than in Zurich. Money was a problem once more. The Mensheviks had managed to wrest control of the Schmitt legacy from Lenin. Moreover, he anticipated that with Russia at war, other sources of funds might be cut off as well. Therefore, in Berne they chose a small, inexpensive apartment. Since Lenin's sister Maria had returned to Russia before the outbreak of hostilities, they only needed room for themselves and Nadezhda's aged mother.

For the time being their sole income was a legacy of four thousand rubles left to Nadezhda by an aunt. They watched their meager funds carefully. Nevertheless, Lenin could not have been happier, for he saw in the war the beginning of the inevitable end of capitalism.

Lenin knew Russia was ill prepared for war. Her industrial development was too restricted and her armies too poorly organized to sustain a lengthy military conflict. Furthermore, war had come so suddenly that the Russian people had not been psychologically prepared for it. There was no carefully drawn plan for mobilizing the entire resources of the nation.

Thus, Lenin was convinced it was the chance he and his fellow socialists had been waiting for. A determined revolutionary effort would transform the war from one between nations to the predetermined civil struggle beten capitalists and workers.

However, Lenin was soon to learn that the issue was not as simple as he had thought it to be. He was astounded to find that most of the socialists did not share his view of the war at all. Instead of joining together to promote revolution, they chose to support their own homelands! In every nation in Europe the so-called revolutionaries were patriotically backing their governments.

What had happened to internationalism? Where was socialist loyalty to the class struggle? Was nationalism so strong that in times of crises it transcended all other commitments? For Lenin, the answers to these vital questions led only to a deep sense of bitterness and betrayal.

Even George Plekhanov, elder statesman of the Social Democratic Party of Russia, was supporting the Allies against Germany and the other Central Powers. Marxists everywhere were organizing patriotic parades. The younger ones rushed to get into uniform. In many countries, the socialists held party conferences to justify their support of the war effort. Many argued that in backing their own government they were choosing the lesser of two evils. Besides, they asserted that such cooperation now would entitle them to a voice in postwar policy, thus helping to advance the cause of socialism.

Lenin refused to buy these arguments. His loyalty was to international socialist revolution, nothing else. He viewed with disgust what he considered a tragic betrayal of Marxism by its adherents.

At one meeting of Social Democrats in Zurich, Plekhanov reiterated his hopes for a Russian and French victory over the Germans. Lenin leaped up from his seat and angrily denounced him as a hypocritical nationalist and traitor to socialism. Others at the meeting shouted him down. Of a leading Marxist named Karl Kautsky, whom he had formerly admired but who was now a leading supporter of the Allied cause, Lenin wrote bitterly: "I hate and despise him more than anyone. He is nothing but a beastly, rotten, sneaking hypocrite."

Lenin, however, was almost alone in his beliefs. Only a few hardcore Bolsheviks such as Inessa Armand still counted themselves among his followers. The realization that so many had deserted the cause turned him into a grim and angry man. Although hooted down at meeting after meeting, he continued to denounce the "lies of the warmakers" and the treason of the socialists who supported them. Only a continuing fanatical belief that the war would ultimately cause nation-states to collapse and make it easier for Communism to take power managed to sustain him.

In the spring of 1915, Nadezhda's mother died. Toward the end she had suffered from chronic ailments and was almost senile. Shortly afterward, the Lenins went to Zurich to live. Desperately low in funds, they rented a single room in a house owned by a shoemaker named Kammerer. The room was small and drab. In hot weather there was an unbelievable stench from a sausage factory across the street. The entire furnishings consisted of a table, two beds, two chairs and a sewing machine. But since the rent was low they found the place tolerable.

The war went on month after month, yet the capitalist nations refused to collapse. Out of habit Lenin continued to attend meetings and make speeches, but his despair grew as his hopes for a massive uprising by the proletariat dimmed.

In July 1916, Lenin received word from Russia that his mother had died. The passing of the aged Maria Alexandrovna Ulyanov was a painful blow. She had protected him through every conceivable crisis. Even when they had been separated by a thousand miles, she had, in a sense, been at his side supporting him either with money or with letters of encouragement. Heartbroken, Lenin spent many days taking long walks in the mountains, feeling more alone than at any time in his life.

It was a moment of despondency and personal defeat. As the year 1916 drew to a close, Lenin was almost on the verge of giving up hope in the revolution. Addressing a group of youthful Swiss laborers in Zurich, he declared: "We, the old ones, may never live to see the decisive battles of the coming revolution."

Curiously Lenin, in his profound despair, had failed to recognize the advance warning of an explosion in Russia that was to rock the world.

11.

The March Revolution

THE ORDEAL OF WAR soon threatened Russia's very survival. The nation was not prepared for a major conflict. In the first days of the war the massive Russian armies, benefiting from weight of numbers, made impressive gains on the Austro-Hungarian front. But late in August 1914 the Tsar's troops suffered a disastrous defeat at the hands of the Germans at Tannenberg.

The military setback affected morale in the armed forces and on the home front. The spirit of the Russian people never recovered.

With a quarter of the male population of working age under arms, a severe labor shortage developed. Food supplies dwindled as millions of acres of farm land went uncultivated. The railroads, lacking skilled help, failed to deliver supplies on time, thereby contributing to the economic crisis. For millions of Russians, hunger and deprivation became a way of life.

New defeats at the hands of the Germans intensified the nation's problems. Vast amounts of artillery and ammunition were lost as the enemy overran Russian territory and captured supply depots and railway freight cars. By the end of 1915 many infantrymen were being sent into battle without arms—under orders to obtain rifles from dead comrades! As a result of her defeats, Russia suffered more than two million casualties. Another million men were taken prisoner by the Germans. Morale sank so swiftly that Russian officers could not be sure their troops would obey a command if given.

Desperate times seemed to call for desperate measures. As 1915 drew to a close, the Tsar announced that he would take personal command of the Army. The move was instigated by strong-willed Empress Alix. Until now, the Army had been under the command of the Grand Duke Nicholas, the Tsar's uncle. Alix bitterly resented the Grand Duke because he despised her spiritual adviser, Rasputin, and did not conceal his contempt. She insisted that her husband take the supreme command away from his uncle on the ground that the Grand Duke was responsible for Russia's military defeats. She argued that by holding the command himself, the Tsar would restore the people's faith in the government and the Army.

Nicholas finally assented. But the move proved to have just the opposite effect of what was intended. The spirit of the troops and those at home sank even lower. Few really believed in the Army's ability to turn the tide of war on the eastern front. Fewer still had faith in the Tsar's competence as a leader.

The change of command had other adverse results. With Nicholas' attention turned to military affairs, governmental decisions increasingly fell to Alix—and through her to Rasputin. In spite of his political ignorance and reactionary outlook, the Empress turned to him more and more for advice. At her request the harried and preoccupied Nicholas dismissed and replaced dozens of government officials in accordance with Rasputin's wishes.

When the Tsar finally left to go to the front, Alix took over virtually all the reins of rule. Rasputin was thus raised to a position of power unmatched by any other man in Russia. He was constantly at the Empress' side, offering advice on policy, making recommendations on appointments and urging harsh treatment of any who dared to oppose her. At his recommendation, she dismissed the Duma because of criticism voiced by some deputies. Any official who even dared to question her decisions was immediately removed. All replacements had to be screened and approved by Rasputin.

Before long, the influence of the self-proclaimed holy man even extended to military strategy. Alix ordered that battle plans be brought to Rasputin so he could review and bless them. His suggestions were then transmitted to the Tsar at the front.

"Do listen to him who only wants your good and whom God has given more insight, wisdom and enlightenment than all the military put together," she once wrote to her husband about Rasputin. "His love for you and Russia is so intense and God has sent him to be your help and guide."

Opposition to Rasputin's seemingly endless influence grew steadily. There was seething anger and resentment within Army and governmental circles. While much of the antagonism remained hidden, a few spoke out candidly. One of these was the Grand Duke Nicholas, who had chosen to remain at the front even after the Tsar had taken over supreme command. Once, Rasputin sent word that he planned to visit the front lines to bless the troops. The Grand Duke telegraphed the following reply: "DARE TO COME TO GENERAL HEADQUARTERS AND I WILL SEE YOU HANGED LIKE A DOG."

The widening repression on the home front was matched by ever-growing losses on the battlefields. As the German armies advanced relentlessly, masses of Russian soldiers deserted. Others feigned illness or surrendered without firing a shot at the approaching enemy. Civilian populations of whole villages and towns fled eastward in panic. Food was in critical short supply, and in Moscow people were reported to be starving.

In some cities the public utilities, such as electrical plants and water pumping stations, were closed down because qualified men were not available to operate them. In many factories the hungry, despairing workers simply walked off the job.

Sensing disaster, the Duma delegates reconvened to plead for desperately needed reforms. Evidence of corruption on the part of high government officials was disclosed. The Duma warned that unless emergency measures were taken, the government was in danger of collapsing. Even members of the nobility added their voices to the growing clamor for reform. But these efforts had little effect. Alix and the Tsar were stubbornly oblivious to every recommendation. It was as if they were determined to prepare the way for revolution.

On the evening of December 16, 1916, the opposition to Rasputin's sinister influence boiled over. A group of nobles, alarmed by the catastrophic direction in which Russia seemed to be heading, took matters into their own hands. One of the conspirators, Prince Yusupov, invited the holy man to a party at his home. There he served the unwary guest cakes and wine containing enough deadly poison to kill a dozen men. When the poison failed to take effect, the drunken Rasputin was shot. His body was then carried to a frozen river and thrust under the ice. Later, when the body was recovered, an autopsy was performed. The examination disclosed that his death was due to drowning, not bullets!

The sensational news of the killing occasioned few expressions of regret. The royal palace was one of the few places where tears were shed. At Alix's insistence, Rasputin was buried near the family chapel at one of the imperial palaces.

Even the warning implicit in Rasputin's murder failed to shake the obstinate refusal of the royal couple to hear the anguished cries of the people. A coalition of moderate political parties again begged the Tsar to institute reforms—if only to help the country prosecute the war more effectively. The proposal was rejected out-of-hand by Nicholas. Moreover, Alix seemed to lose touch with reality altogether. Despondent over the death of Rasputin, she began holding seances to contact his spirit for advice on government policy!

By this time the peasants, workers and radicals were no longer alone in their alienation from the government. They had been joined by the conservative middle class—the people of wealth, power and education.

Even the secret police were now nervously anticipating widespread domestic trouble. In January 1917 they reported to the Tsar that the people were on the brink of revolt and were demanding either food or an end to the war.

The Duma met the following month. Its members passed a resolution stating its determination not to be dismissed by the Tsar. Then one of the deputies of the moderate Labor Party, Alexander Kerensky, warned that only Nicholas' removal from the throne could save Russia. When the Empress heard about it she snapped that Kerensky deserved to be hanged.

By March 1917 the stage was set for revolution.

Shop windows were empty. The food situation was more critical than at any time since the beginning of the war. Bakeries put up signs reading, "There is no bread today." The temper of the Russian people was one of despair and blind, helpless rage at a government that had ceased to have any meaning for them. The Duma president, a conservative politician named Rodzianko, wired the Tsar at Army headquarters in a last desperate attempt to secure reforms. After reading the message, Nicholas observed, "That fat Rodzianko has written me some nonsense to which I shall not even reply."

As the nation was propelled toward revolution the exiled revolutionaries were conspicuous by their absence and silence. Like Lenin, most failed to recognize the symptoms of an upheaval that was only days away. The Leninist theory maintained that revolutions were planned by a small, elite corps of professional leaders. The notion that the masses, by themselves, could reach a point of spontaneous revolt was alien to the Bolshevik philosophy. Yet that was precisely the state of things in Russia. Tsarism was about to collapse because, for the masses, it had become the symbolic source of all the death, misery and hunger caused by the war. There was no organized attempt at rebellion, no conspiracy to undermine the tsarist government. What was about to take place was the most spontaneous revolution in the history of the world.

During the first days in March (late February under the Julian calendar which was in use in Russia until 1918) thousands of housewives in St. Petersburg milled around the empty, locked shops demanding bread. On March 8 masses of workers deserted their factories to join the women in the streets. By the following day, the crowds had grown to more than two hundred thousand. The police called for troops from the St. Petersburg army garrison to help control the people. Instead of dispersing the mobs, the troops joined them!

Confused and uncomprehending, Empress Alix wrote to her husband: "Boys and girls are racing around shouting that they have no bread in order to create excitement."

The strikes and riots spread across Russia like a brush fire. The Tsar blandly decided that it was the politicians who were stirring up the people. "DISSOLVE THE DUMA," he wired Duma president Rodzianko imperiously.

In keeping with its earlier resolution, the Duma refused to dissolve. Instead the delegates voted in favor of Alexander Kerensky's demand that the Tsar abdicate. By now even the Empress was beginning to sense the seriousness of the situation. She sent Nicholas a message warning that "CONCESSIONS ARE NECESSARY."

Meanwhile, with the nation in ferment, the old St. Petersburg Soviet, established in 1905 as a council of various labor groups, was quickly revived. The workers were soon joined by thousands of deserting soldiers, including in some instances entire regiments.

No longer able to ignore reality, the Tsar suddenly decided he had no choice but to abdicate. He boarded the imperial train at Army headquarters and ordered it to proceed to St. Petersburg. On March 15, as the train neared the capital, it ground to a halt at a siding near the town of Pskov. There, with two members of the Duma present, the Tsar announced he was turning over the throne to his brother, the Grand Duke Michael.

It was already too late. The news of Nicholas' abdication was greeted by a general denunciation of tsardom and autocracy. The people no longer could be appeased with a gesture. "We want no more Romanovs!" the St. Petersburg Soviet declared. "We want a republic!"

In the Duma, a Provisional Committee was set up to head the government. The Grand Duke Michael, more astute than his brother, turned down the offer of the crown. He stated that he was supporting the Duma's Provisional Committee. Thus, three centuries of rule by the Romanov tsars had come to an end.

The Provisional Committee was now established as the Provisional Government of Russia. Responding to the demand for political reforms it immediately proclaimed freedom of speech, press and assembly; the workers' right to organize and strike; the abolition of all discrimination based on class or nationality; election instead of appointment of officials to local governments; the creation of a Constituent Assembly to decide the form of government for the future. Delegates to the assembly were to be chosen by universal suffrage based on a direct, secret ballot.

In Zurich, Lenin—who recently had expressed doubt that revolution would come in his lifetime—was caught off guard by the monumental events. News of the bread riots had failed to reach the Swiss papers. As a result, he first learned of the establishment of a Provisional Government from a Polish friend who rushed into the apartment shouting, "Have you heard the news? There's a revolution in Russia!" The accounts of the Russian upheaval and the Tsar's abdication continued to be fragmentary. Nevertheless, once it was clear that the impossible had happened—a revolution without professional revolutionaries—Lenin was caught up in a fever pitch of excitement. He sensed with a kind of messianic fervor that this was to be *his* revolution.

Recalling the bitter experience of 1905, Lenin resolved not to be an absentee revolutionary again. He decided that somehow he must get to Russia at once. But how? With all of Europe in flames, there was little hope of his leaving "this accursed Switzerland" in the near future.

Meanwhile, he telephoned, telegraphed and wrote to his Bolshevik comrades, urging them to exploit the situation in Russia at all costs. The Bolsheviks, he warned, must immediately embark on a propaganda campaign "for an *international* proletarian revolution and for the conquest of power."

From Lenin's standpoint, what had taken place in Russia was not the real revolution at all, merely a first step. According to Marxist dogma the bourgeoisie must overthrow the feudal autocracy before the stage could be set for an authentic socialist revolution. Now that the capitalists had gotten rid of the Tsar, the next step in the Marxist progression must be implemented—the revolt of the proletarian masses against bourgeois capitalism.

In reply to a telegram from a Bolshevik colleague asking for instructions, Lenin wrote:

> Our immediate task is to broaden the scope of our work, to organize the masses, to arouse new social strata, the backward elements, the rural population, the domestic servants, to form nuclei in the army for the purpose of carrying on a systematic and detailed exposé of the government, to prepare for the seizure of power by the Soviets.

To Lenin and his Bolsheviks, the Provisional Government had replaced the Tsar as the enemy of the people. Therefore every effort must be made to undermine the fledgling government so that the socialists could wrest power away from it. From the standpoint of strategy, Lenin saw in the revived soviets—the workers' councils—the ideal weapon to accomplish this task. The soviets were the only organizations with enough popular strength to take power from the Provisional Government. In 1905 he had seen how easy it was for an effective politician such as Leon Trotsky to become a leading figure in the soviets. Thus, if a split could be effected between the soviets and the Provisional Government, the way might be opened for a Bolshevik coup.

What was alien to Lenin's thinking was the concept that the Duma deputies who ran the Provisional Government could be honestly interested in helping the people. It never occurred to him that they might be truly dedicated to the task of establishing a representative democracy in Russia. To the committed Marxist who viewed society solely in terms of a power struggle between the classes, such a notion was incomprehensible.

While feverishly planning his political strategy, Lenin continued to explore every possibility for getting to Russia. At night he lay awake devising involved schemes. He dreamed of finding an airplane that could fly him over the front lines to Petrograd—the new name for St. Petersburg.

Another scheme called for him to assume the identity of a friend with a British passport. Since the friend had hair and Lenin was bald, he would wear a wig. He would then make his way to England, take a boat to Sweden and finally reach Russia.

While Lenin was wracking his brain for a way to Petrograd, other revolutionaries were doing the same. In Geneva, a number of Russian exiles held a meeting to consider various ideas. One was a proposal by Lenin's old enemy Jules Martov. He boldly suggested that the German government be contacted directly and asked to provide safe conduct for a group of Russian exiles across Germany. Since the exiles were in favor of discontinuing the war, the benefit to Germany could be great.

Martov's idea was so fantastic that the others quickly dismissed it as impractical. But several days later, a friend reported it to Lenin. The outrageous audacity of the scheme appealed to him. In any case it was worth a try. The Germans would undoubtedly listen to any proposal that might end the war on the eastern front, thereby releasing many regiments for the west.

Through friends, Lenin arranged for the plan to be submitted to the German embassy in Berne. From there it was passed along to high authorities in Berlin.

While awaiting an answer, Lenin was not idle. He wrote a series of letters for publication in *Pravda* in which he attempted to set the stage for the second uprising—the socialist revolution. He knew that everything depended on speed. If the Bolsheviks were to succeed at all, they must wrest control while the Provisional Government was still weak and unsettled. Through the soviets, particularly the Petrograd Soviet, the proletariat must be stirred to rise against the new government.

Accordingly, in his article for *Pravda*, which he entitled "Letters from Afar," Lenin kept hammering away at a single theme. The masses needed *peace, bread and freedom,* he wrote. He recognized that this slogan dramatized what was of greatest concern to the Russian masses. The nation was bleeding from war, and the people were sick and tired of fighting. Yet the provisional leaders had pledged to continue the war "for freedom in the world." The new government was composed of political moderates such as George Lvov and Alexander Kerensky, who felt a keen sense of loyalty to the Allied cause. They believed that in order to survive as a democracy, Russia would need the recognition and strong support of her democratic allies. The suggestion that she pull out of the war struck them as cowardly and dishonorable, a policy designed to alienate Russia from her friends.

The issue of bread was also a critical one. In the few weeks since the establishment of the Provisional Government, there had hardly been time to improve the desperate food situation.

Finally, Lenin sought to convince the people that the freedoms already established were in reality a sham. The fact that the Provisional Government had instituted democratic policies as advanced as any in the world made no impact on him. As long as Russia was under the control of bourgeois leaders, it was simply another form of enslavement of the masses, he insisted.

Early in April, the Germans replied to Lenin's proposal. They informed him through intermediaries that the plan had been approved. Under the agreement Lenin and a handful of fellow exiles would be carried by "sealed train" through Germany into Sweden. The journey would be undertaken with the full knowledge and cooperation of the German government. Once in Sweden, the exiles would make their way to Petrograd.

Lenin was beside himself with excitement and joy. Soon he would have his revolution.

12.

At the Finland Station

IN APPROVING the strange journey, the Germans knew exactly what they were doing. German intelligence officers were well informed on conditions in Russia. They had also collected detailed dossiers on many of the exiles. The strategy of the Kaiser's generals was to bring the war on the Russian front to an early end so they could concentrate on the western front. If this could be accomplished by political intrigue rather than by force of arms, so much the better. Furthermore, the Germans reasoned that no one was better equipped to exploit the war-weariness of the Russians than Lenin and his Bolsheviks.

On the afternoon of April 9, 1917, everything was ready. Lenin, Nadezhda, Inessa Armand and about thirty other Russian exiles gathered at the railroad station in Berne waiting to board their train. Many carried baskets, hampers or brown paper parcels of food. Under other circumstances they might have been mistaken for a party of picnickers. Not today. Lenin had hoped for a quiet and unnoticed departure, but news of the journey had leaked out. An angry crowd of prowar Russian émigrés gathered at the station waving banners and shouting insults at the revolutionaries.

In defiance, the departing exiles began to sing the "Internationale," anthem of the revolutionary movement. A near-riot broke out. There were shouts of "German spies!" and "The Kaiser is paying for your trip!" from the anti-Bolsheviks. The din was so loud that Lenin's people were forced to break off their singing.

Finally, after a good deal of pushing and shoving, they managed to board their car. At 3:10 P.M., the train slid slowly out of the Berne station. As it picked up speed, it passed fields already turning green under the touch of an early Swiss spring. They sped past small villages and clear blue mountain lakes in their headlong dash toward the German frontier.

At the border of Switzerland and Germany, Swiss custom officials examined their belongings and confiscated all their food supplies, particularly chocolate and sugar. When they rolled across the frontier, the German officials abruptly ordered them out of the train. They were kept waiting in a customs shed for half an hour without an explanation. Some of the exiles wondered anxiously whether the Germans had tricked them and planned to arrest or shoot them. Lenin said nothing and stood off by himself with Nadezhda and Inessa at his side.

At last they were told to board the train once more. Still no reason had been given for the mysterious delay. When they finally pulled away from the border station many breathed a nervous sigh of relief.

Although the train was known as a "sealed train" it was not actually padlocked. Lenin's agreement with the German government called for the exiles to have no contact with the population while the train was passing through Germany. In this sense they were to be "sealed off" from outside communication whenever the train paused to take on coal or supplies.

Lenin saw to it that the group kept its side of the bargain. Not a word was exchanged between the exiles and Germans during the frequent stops. In return, the German train crew treated them well. They were supplied with newspapers and beer which they consumed in great quantities.

During the long slow journey Lenin and Nadezhda occupied a small private compartment. The other exiles agreed that Lenin, as their acknowledged leader, deserved privacy so he could think and work without interruption. Nevertheless, he was kept aware of their presence by the strong odor of tobacco fumes that assaulted his eyes and nose. Many of the Bolsheviks were chain smokers, and the unventilated carriage was thick with clouds of cigarette smoke. Nonsmoker Lenin complained angrily to Nadezhda that he was being suffocated.

The exile train chugged slowly through German villages and towns that were eerily silent and unanimated. The people stared with expressionless faces at the train but did not wave or smile. The population seemed composed almost exclusively of old people or young people. There were few young or middle-aged men. The war had drained Germany of its youth. Even the farms and fields were worked by the elderly.

The meals provided aboard the train were excellent. They were in sharp contrast to the pathetic drabness the exiles saw all around them as they gazed through the train windows. Clearly, the Germans were trying to give the impression they were a nation on the road to victory. But the revolutionaries had been too long familiar with the poverty that existed in Russia to be fooled.

After four weary days of travel, they reached the north German town of Sassnitz. The long journey in the sealed train was over. The exiles took a ferryboat to Sweden, then got a train to the nearby city of Malmö. Here a group of Swedish Social Democrats greeted them as conquering heroes. A smorgasbord feast was prepared and they ate and relaxed for a few hours before proceeding on to Stockholm.

In the Swedish capital Lenin engaged in a whirlwind of activity. He bought armloads of books, held meetings with Russian exiles who had been living in Sweden and shopped with Nadezhda for some much needed clothing.

When they finally boarded the train for the long journey to Russia, Lenin did not hide his impatience. Almost as soon as they pulled out of the station he began muttering about the slow speed of the locomotive. The trip around the Gulf of Bothnia was painfully long and there were frequent stops. At the border between Sweden and Finland, they were delayed while soldiers interrogated each passenger. However, by the time the journey was resumed, Lenin's mood had changed. Since Finland belonged to Russia, he could not help feeling that they were already home. Even the presence of Russian soldiers was a pleasing sight.

At the town of Belo-Ostrov, on the frontier of Finland and Russia, they paused again for customs inspection. Here, Lenin was amazed to find a crowd of about a hundred workmen milling about the station platform and shouting his name—"Len-in! Len-in!" Yet even this pleasant and unexpected reception did not prepare him for what he was to find in the capital itself.

They arrived in Petrograd on the night of April 16. It was after 11:00 P.M. when the train steamed into the railroad depot—known as the Finland Station. In spite of the late hour, the place was ablaze with bizarre patterns of light formed by huge searchlights from the huge Peter and Paul Fortress close by. Thousands of people carrying banners had come to greet Lenin, and they pressed forward anxiously to catch a first glimpse of the returning Bolshevik leader. The station platform was decorated with red banners. Each arch and doorway was festooned with red and gold ribbon containing revolutionary inscriptions.

The Bolsheviks who had arranged the reception had done their work well. It was almost like a triumphal ceremony. Lenin had not had the slightest hint that anything like this was being prepared for his arrival. Indeed, throughout the journey, he had had a recurring fear that the entire group might be arrested by the Provisional Government the moment they set foot in Petrograd. Instead he was being allowed to return with all the fanfare usually reserved for a conqueror.

Lining the station in front of the crowd were soldiers and sailors standing at stiff attention. An air of tense anticipation gripped the people as the door to the carriage was thrown open. Lenin, small and unprepossessing in his drab, wrinkled clothes, emerged. At that moment a band struck up the "Marseillaise." A smartly dressed young naval officer from the Baltic fleet stepped stiffly forward, saluted and welcomed Lenin to Petrograd. A thunderous roar went up from the crowd. Followed by Nadezhda and the other exiles, he was escorted to the former imperial waiting room. There he was greeted by several members of the Petrograd Soviet who had been waiting for him.

One of the officials, Nikolay Chkeidze, delivered a brief greeting:

> Comrade Lenin, in the name of the Petrograd Soviet of Workers' and Soldiers' Deputies and the whole revolution we welcome you to Russia . . . but we believe that the principal task of the revolutionary democracy at present is to defend our revolution from every kind of attack both from within and from without. We believe that what is needed is not disunity but the closing of the ranks of the entire democracy. We hope you will pursue these aims together with us.

It was an appeal for support of the Provisional Government. In effect, Chkeidze was pleading with the Bolsheviks not to destroy the revolution that had already taken place but to participate in united action.

For Lenin, it was the moment he had been waiting for. Turning contemptuously away from the officials of the Petrograd Soviet, he addressed the crowd in a rasping voice:

> Dear comrades, soldiers, sailors and workers! I am happy to greet in your persons the victorious Russian revolution! I greet you as the vanguard of the world proletarian army. The predatory imperialist war is the beginning of a civil war all over Europe. The hour is not too far off when . . . the people will turn their weapons against the capitalist exploiters. The sun of the world socialist revolution has already risen. In Germany there is a seething ferment. Any day we shall see the collapse of European imperialism. The Russian revolution you have made has prepared the way and opened a new epoch. Long live the world socialist revolution!

He had shouted out those final words, "Long live the world socialist revolution!" The crowd roared them back at him, like a battle cry. He had deliberately ignored Chkeidze's appeal for a statement of unity. Instead he had chosen to speak about the real revolution-to-come, the socialist revolution. And he had managed to hypnotize the crowd, so that they were ready to do his bidding. As they shouted and cheered, Lenin was suffused with the warmth of his newly found power. He smiled broadly for the first time that night. Then he stamped his feet and rocked from side to side in a curious little victory dance as the huge searchlights framed him in a giant circle of light.

Lenin's return proved to be part of a mass influx of exiles and refugees to Russia. The new government had announced amnesties or pardons for political prisoners. Now they returned by the tens of thousands. They came from every corner of Europe and from America, too. They traveled by boat and train and sometimes on foot. It took twenty thousand sleighs to bring back the exiles from northern Siberia alone.

Among those returning were George Plekhanov, Leon Trotsky and Joseph Djugashvili. Djugashvili, who had been in Siberia, now called himself by a new name—*Stalin*, meaning "steel."

The return of the exiles had an immediate political effect. Like Lenin, most sensed the importance of the soviets in the coming struggle for power and hastened to join these workers' councils. Within weeks, the Petrograd Soviet, which had been moderate, drifted toward radicalism. Lenin devoted most of his efforts to trying to drive a wedge between the soviets and the Provisional Government. Although a small faction, the Bolsheviks were more tightly organized and disciplined than the Mensheviks or any of the other groups. Thus, each day found their influence growing.

Lenin was candid about his strategy. He summed it up before a small group of Bolshevik leaders in direct terms. The Bolsheviks should not cooperate with the Provisional Government, he warned. They should not help it fight imperialist war. They should concentrate instead on the real, socialist revolution by converting the imperialist war into a true civil war. This could best be accomplished by gaining control of the soviets and demanding that the Provisional Government's power be surrendered to the soviets. "All Power to the Soviets" must be the Bolshevik slogan. Furthermore, he declared, they would mercilessly attack Mensheviks, liberals and every other faction that refused to support Bolshevik opposition to the Provisional Government and its war policy.

Lenin's policy of straight-out opposition to the war was extremely effective. It had a powerful appeal for a war-weary people who were longing for someone to tell them the fighting must be stopped. By contrast, the Mensheviks and other non-Bolshevik factions were confused and uncertain on the war issue. They saw the importance of having Russia fulfill her commitment to her allies. Yet they were also aware of the antiwar mood of the people. As a result, they failed to take a strong position and vacillated between support and criticism of the Provisional Government's policies.

All during the spring, the Bolshevik campaign to undermine the government gained strength. It was aided and abetted by the apathy, confusion and disorganization of the moderates. The Provisional Government stood almost alone. It was attacked bitterly by its enemies but received little firm support from its friends. Moreover, the government's floundering actions reflected its sense of insecurity. Alexander Kerensky, who was serving as Minister of War, complained in dismay and despair that the government was paralyzed —"it does not work but only discusses its condition."

The Provisional Government, which had ridden to power on a wave of popular support, thus incurred widespread resentment. Some officials complained that the people had expected too much too soon. In point of fact, aside from political reforms, there had been little change in their condition. Most of the economic problems that had plagued the nation under the Tsar were still present. Food was critically short; hunger and misery still abounded; transport and supply facilities were hopelessly snarled. Many Russians claimed that in the five months since the Provisional Government had assumed power, nothing had been accomplished. At the same time they denounced the rules and regulations which Prince Lvov, President of the government, and his ministers introduced to solve the most urgent problems. In many respects it was the reaction of a people unused to democratic government who were convinced that *any* restraints infringed on their freedom.

Yet the most difficult challenge faced by the new government was the war. Minister of War Kerensky, hoping to restore morale and rebuild support for the war, ordered preparations for a major summer offensive. The war's opponents, particularly the Bolsheviks, seized on his plan as excellent ammunition for their antigovernment propaganda. They organized a campaign of regular demonstrations and mass marches. More and more posters began to carry the Bolshevik slogans: "War to the Palaces; Peace to the Huts" and "All Power to the Soviets."

On July 16 and 17, the domestic pressure which had been building up exploded into violence. In Petrograd, the demonstrations were spontaneously transformed into riots and mass disorder. Although the Bolsheviks did not actually direct or lead these outbreaks, they spurred on the angry crowds by shouting "Peace, Land, Bread and Power." Calls by some Mensheviks and other moderates for support of the Provisional Government went unheeded. George Plekhanov, elder statesman of Russian radicalism, was hooted off a speaker's platform after pleading for restraint and unity.

The disorders grew worse. Crowds of workers, soldiers and sailors mobbed the streets of the capital. They echoed the Bolshevik demands for overthrow of the Provisional Government and the seizure of power by the soviets.

For once, the Provisional Government stood firm. Troops were dispatched to deal with the mobs. In a few sectors of the city there were bloody clashes between the government forces and the rioters. The show of strength proved effective. Within hours after the Army was called out, the protesters were dispersed and calm was restored to the city.

It was a disastrous defeat for Lenin and the Bolsheviks. Although they had not led the disorders in any formal sense, they were forced to accept the blame for them. The Bolsheviks who had participated in the riots had been among the most vocal inciters. As a result, they were now the most easily identifiable. Lenin's unrelenting attacks on the Provisional Government in the past lent weight to the belief that it had been a Bolshevik-controlled uprising designed to seize power.

The case against Lenin seemed to be clinched by the publication of documents alleging that he was a German agent! Rumors had circulated all along about the mysterious "sealed train" trip through Germany. Many Russians had been asking themselves quietly, why would the Germans permit such a thing unless Lenin was indeed their agent? Now the vague suspicions seemed to be bolstered by documentary evidence. Among the published information was a strong hint that the Bolsheviks had received money from the Germans to finance their antigovernment activities.

Some of the documents were later shown to be forgeries. Nevertheless, there was just enough truth in the allegations concerning Lenin's arrangements with the Germans to damn him. What had earlier been whispered was now voiced aloud. There was a public clamor against Lenin and the Bolsheviks. War Minister Alexander Kerensky issued orders for Lenin's immediate arrest and the seizure of Bolshevik headquarters.

Only three months before, at the Finland Station, Lenin had been welcomed as a returning hero. Now he was a hunted man again with a police warrant out against him. He and Nadezhda agreed that he must go into hiding. Lenin donned a borrowed raincoat, put on his peaked cap and left the apartment where they had been living.

During the next few days hundreds of Bolsheviks were arrested. A major topic of conversation throughout Petrograd was the imminent arrest of "traitor Lenin." Despite his mysterious disappearance the city was rife with rumors that the police knew his whereabouts and would soon have him in custody. But as the days wore on, Lenin seemed to have vanished from Petrograd and indeed from Russia itself.

In the working-class districts of Petrograd, few persons seemed to notice the presence of a small, unobtrusive middle-aged workman who called himself Konstantin Ivanov. He wore an ill-fitting raincoat and a peaked cap pulled down over his eyes. Except for several Bolshevik leaders who were aware of Ivanov's real identity, no one seemed to recognize the mild-mannered little man as the fugitive Vladimir Lenin.

13.

The November Revolution

BY LATE SUMMER the Provisional Government was in trouble. The big offensive against the Germans had failed miserably; troop morale was lower than ever. Although the July uprising had been quelled, domestic unrest continued. Frustrated and discouraged, Prince Lvov resigned as President of the Provisional Government. He was succeeded by Alexander Kerensky.

Kerensky was youthful, brilliant and outgoing. By a curious coincidence, he was from Lenin's own hometown of Simbirsk. His father was Feodor Kerensky, the same gentle schoolmaster whose recommendation had gotten Lenin into the University of Kazan law school thirty years earlier! However, the younger Kerensky and Lenin had not known each other.

While the new President had intelligence and energy, the problems facing him were too formidable to be solved overnight. He was soon plagued by conservatives who complained bitterly of the confusion and anarchy in Russia. They charged that the government was too irresolute to cope with the situation.

To appease these groups, Kerensky appointed General Lavr Kornilov, a favorite of the conservative elements, as Commander-in-Chief of the armed forces. Although a brave soldier, Kornilov was not an astute politician. He immediately aroused the ire of the liberals and radicals by dissolving "soldiers' committees" which the Provisional

Government had established to give the troops a voice. At the same time, he called for the soviets to be disbanded and the Bolsheviks to be hanged!

Kerensky soon saw that the Kornilov appointment had been a mistake. His fears grew when he heard reports that the General was planning to seize the government and set himself up as a dictator. Moreover, as the military situation worsened, there was speculation that the Germans might ultimately reach Petrograd.

Faced with these threats, Kerensky's first step was to protect the royal family. Following the Tsar's abdication, Nicholas, Alix and their children had been kept in protective custody at a royal palace nearby. Kerensky now had them transferred to western Siberia for their own safety.

Next, he decided to rally public support against Kornilov. The General was already massing troops to march on Petrograd. But here Kerensky was in a dilemma. He needed all the help he could get, and the Bolshevik faction was one of the few groups sufficiently organized and disciplined to oppose Kornilov effectively. But to release them from prison so they could form the spearhead of defense was risky. Kerensky was well aware that the Bolsheviks' ultimate goal was to destroy the Provisional Government. Yet in the face of the immediate threat from Kornilov, was there any choice?

Still in hiding, Lenin managed to keep in close touch with the events in Petrograd. From the capital, friends had smuggled him by freight train to the village of Razliv where he shaved off his beard. For many days he lived in the fields, subsisting on tea and potatoes, which he suspended on forked sticks over a small fire. Each day messengers brought him news from Petrograd.

As the end of August approached, the weather turned cool and Lenin could no longer remain outdoors. Arrangements were made to smuggle him across the border into Finland in the cab of a train engine.

He ended up in the Finnish town of Helsingfors. The chief of police there was a Bolshevik sympathizer named Gustav Rovio, who had been elected to office following the March revolution. Informed of Lenin's arrival, Rovio met him secretly. Since Rovio's wife was away in the country, he invited Lenin to live in his apartment! The offer was gratefully accepted. What safer place could he find than the apartment of the chief of police?

In the following weeks, Lenin spent his time preparing a manuscript entitled *The State and Revolution*. It was an attempt to grapple with the problem of what would happen *after* the socialist revolution. Until now, he had concentrated on the mechanics of revolution. But after the revolution, what?

The works of Marx and Engels offered little information on this point, except for vague references to the "withering away of the state." In one of his works, Engels had written that "when there is no longer any class to be held in subjection, then state interference in social relations becomes, in one domain after another, superfluous, and then withers away of itself, the government of persons being replaced by the administration of things and by the conduct of processes of production."

In truth, Lenin was perplexed by Engels' vision. As propaganda, the notion of the state's demise could be useful since it appealed to the antiauthoritarian sentiment of the masses. But when he examined the practical implications of such a concept, he was riddled with doubt and hesitancy. Was it really possible for the state to "wither away"? If so, how long would it take? Could all the tasks now performed by government actually be reduced to the simple administrative and bookkeeping functions which Engels had envisioned?

In the end, Lenin was unable to come up with any profound answers. He concluded unhappily that the withering-away process, if it were to be realized at all, would be a long and protracted one. Yet at the same time, he recognized the practical need to provide his own followers, as well as the masses, with an appealing vision of a socialist utopia.

When completed, *The State and Revolution* was a primitive, simplistic picture of the future. In the process of revolution, Lenin wrote, the state would be totally smashed. Replacing it would be a utopian kind of society in which all wealth and private property would be abolished. In this way there would be nothing which one man could acquire that would be coveted by another. All needs would be provided for by a central distributing agency. Everyone would be employed by the state and would receive the same salary, whether factory worker or government official. The central task of government would thus be "the extraordinarily simple operations of watching, recording and issuing receipts, and these are [functions] within the reach of anybody who can read and write and knows the first four rules of arithmetic." The government would not pass laws or impose regulations because these would no longer be necessary.

In reducing the role of the state to that of a giant calculating machine, Lenin was satisfied that he had provided sufficient guidelines for the present. Privately, he continued to harbor nagging doubts about many aspects of the vision, particularly about the timetable for this massive transformation of society. But he finally convinced himself that once the revolution took place there would be time enough to work out the structural details. The crucial issue at the moment was the socialist revolution itself.

In Helsingfors, Lenin continued to receive daily reports on the situation in Petrograd. He was delighted to hear of Kerensky's dilemma involving Kornilov. Should the Provisional Government decide to release the Bolshevik prisoners and arm the people to meet the Kornilov threat, the stage would be set for revolution. With guns, the masses, led by the Bolsheviks, would have little difficulty toppling Kerensky, Lenin told himself.

Others, including the more moderate Bolsheviks, argued that according to Marxist doctrine, the time was not yet right. Since the bourgeois revolution was not completed, a socialist revolution was premature and almost certainly doomed to failure. Lenin, however, was not troubled by ideological considerations. Believing that ideology should be exploited, not venerated, he was infuriated by the reluctance of some of his fellow leaders. The important thing, he warned, was to seize opportunity where it could be found. To lose this chance might mean the indefinite postponing of the revolution.

In spite of his disgust with some of his fellow Bolsheviks, Lenin was heartened by one development. Leon Trotsky, formerly a leading Menshevik, had begun to change his thinking. Since returning to Petrograd in the spring, he had drawn closer to Lenin's concepts and had adopted many Bolshevik ideas. A participant in the July riots, Trotsky was one of those arrested after the failure of the summer uprising. Since the former Menshevik wielded great influence in the Petrograd Soviet, Lenin knew that his support would be of crucial significance when the revolution began.

Early in September, President Kerensky arrived at a critical decision. He would release the arrested Bolsheviks and arm them and the Petrograd workers through the soviet, so that the capital could be defended against Kornilov.

As they streamed out of the jails, the Bolsheviks lost no time in seizing the initiative. Among those released was Trotsky, who was almost immediately elected Chairman of the Petrograd Soviet. A new "Committee to Fight Counterrevolution" was established by the Bolsheviks and the Soviet to plan joint strategy. Trotsky persuaded the other members of the Soviet to give legal sanction to a new militia known as the Red Guard. The Bolsheviks had begun to organize the Guard secretly in anticipation of such a situation. Now, with the Soviet's blessing, it was transformed into a full-fledged military unit armed with rifles and machine guns supplied by the Provisional Government. Within weeks, the Red Guard swelled to more than twenty-five thousand men, including many soldiers and sailors who had deserted their regular units.

Members of the Guard were dispatched to infiltrate Kornilov's army and spread discontent and fear among his troops. Others set up street barricades in Petrograd, in case he invaded the capital.

The assault that Kerensky had feared never came to pass. By the time General Kornilov was ready to march on the Provisional Government, his army had virtually disintegrated. Through the effective propaganda work of the Red Guard agents his troops deserted him by the thousands. Reduced in the end to a handful of men, Kornilov decided to call off his campaign. Kerensky immediately ordered him relieved of his command and had him arrested.

Although the threat from the right had been averted, there was a new and growing danger from the left. In a few short weeks, the militant, disciplined Bolsheviks, though still small in numbers, had gained growing power and influence. They now controlled the Petrograd Soviet and had an army of twenty-five thousand at their disposal. Moreover, they were making inroads in other soviets, including the one in Moscow.

Nevertheless Kerensky was still forced to turn to the left for help.

Since the threat of a German invasion was real, he asked the Bolsheviks to join in defending the country from the enemy. From his refuge in Finland, Lenin wrote an article making the Bolshevik position clear. The Bolsheviks would continue their agitation against Kerensky and the government, he declared. Further, they would defend Russia *"only after* the transfer of power to the proletariat, *after* the offer of peace, *after* the renunciation of secret [international] treaties and of the ties with the banks, *only after."* Not even the capture of Petrograd itself would move the Bolsheviks to participate in an imperialist war and defend a bourgeois government, he thundered.

Lenin found his enforced absence from the center of political activity in Petrograd increasingly trying. The fear that he might once again miss the start of revolution, as he had in 1905 and the previous March, brought him near the point of nervous exhaustion. But the warrant for his arrest had not yet been withdrawn. Accordingly, his fellow Bolsheviks worried that he would be taken into custody as soon as he set foot in Russia.

Late in September, Lenin arrived at a crucial decision. Impressed by reports of the political strides the Bolsheviks had made, he decided that the exact time for the socialist revolution had arrived. Given the weakness of Kerensky's government and the newly acquired influence of the Bolsheviks, he was convinced there would never be a more propitious moment to launch an insurrection. And if that were to happen, he, Lenin, wanted to be as close to the scene as possible.

On September 30, he donned a wig and took a train to Vyborg, just inside the Finnish frontier. There, only a few miles from Petrograd itself, he was given shelter in the apartment of a Finnish journalist named Latukk.

As soon as word reached the Bolshevik leadership in Petrograd that Lenin was "next door," an official named Shotman was sent to meet with him. Lenin announced his belief that the time for revolution had arrived. Shotman was startled at the abruptness of the announcement. Sensing his skepticism, Lenin showed him tables of statistics which he had carefully prepared, showing a tremendous growth in Bolshevik strength.

"The country is for us," Lenin declared with absolute conviction. "That is why our chief task at this moment is the immediate organization of all of our forces to take over power."

Shotman protested that even if this could be accomplished, they lacked the experts to run the machinery of government. "Pure absurdity!" Lenin retorted confidently. "Any workman can learn to become a minister in a few days. There is no need for any special ability. It is not even necessary that he should understand the technicalities. That side of things will be done by the functionaries who will be forced to work for us."

Two weeks later, Lenin returned to Petrograd. He was still beardless and using the name Konstantin Ivanov. In addition, his disguise consisted of spectacles and a wig, and one of his friends observed that he looked like a middle-aged Lutheran minister. A loyal party member named Margarita Fofanova offered to put him up in her apartment in a residential suburb. Although Nadezhda was told of his arrival, it was agreed that a reunion would be too risky for the time being.

On the night of October 23, the leadership, or Central Committee, of the Bolshevik faction held a secret meeting that was to have momentous consequences for Russia and the world.

The conclave took place in the apartment of a party member named Nikolay Sukhanov. Called on short notice at Lenin's request, it was attended by only twelve of the twenty-one members of the Central Committee. Lenin arrived last, disguised in his wig and spectacles. The others present included Trotsky and Stalin.

The meeting began in relaxed, friendly fashion over sandwiches and tea served by Mrs. Sukhanov. The chairman, Yakov Swerdlov, read several reports. Then Lenin took the floor amid ominous silence. His words were clear, straightforward, dramatic in their simplicity. The time had come for an uprising, he declared. It must take place *now*. There could be no delay. The opportunity was ripe for a seizure of power. There must be no failure of will. "We dare not wait, we dare not delay," he warned again and again.

The meeting lasted ten hours. The committee members voiced deep-seated fears. They doubted that they had enough strength to carry out an insurrection. They reminded Lenin of how easily the Provisional Government had put down the July riots.

To these arguments, Lenin replied angrily that to reject the chance for revolution would be cowardly and irresponsible. Tacitly, he accused the Central Committee of lacking courage and foresight. Then he launched into brutal attacks on individual members for sounding like "traitors to the revolution."

Lenin brooked no opposition. Armed with iron-clad determination, he did not mince words nor hide the fact that he was out to impose his will on the Committee.

After hours of wavering, most of the others gave in. By a vote of ten to two, the Central Committee endorsed an armed uprising. Yet though he had emerged victorious, Lenin did not exult. On the contrary, he felt wearied and infuriated by the waste of time over a proposition that seemed to him eminently clear and reasonable. Moreover, the two committee members who had opposed him to the last were Lev Kamenev and Grigory Zinoviev. Because both had been among his strongest supporters, Lenin felt a special sense of dismay at what he considered an act of personal and political betrayal. He could not forgive them for this.

A seven-member Politburo (Political Bureau) was established to serve as the high command of the projected revolution. In addition to Lenin, the members included Trotsky, Stalin, Zinoviev, Kamenev, Grigory Solkolnikov and Andrey Bubnov. Trotsky occupied an especially strategic position. Not only was he President of the Petrograd Soviet, but he had just been elected Chairman of its new Military Revolutionary Committee. Since the Committee's task was to organize the defense of Petrograd against "counterrevolution," Bolshevik control of the Petrograd Soviet was now virtually absolute. Soviets in cities across Russia had similarly been "taken over" by disciplined Leninists.

During the next two weeks, the Bolsheviks, under orders of the Central Committee, worked feverishly to build up revolutionary sentiment among the people. Mass support seemed to grow daily.

Meanwhile, the Kerensky government remained in a state of virtual paralysis. It was seemingly incapable of taking action even to protect itself. Rumors of the Bolshevik plot reached Kerensky, but he found it hard to believe that the small faction would dare to attempt an uprising. Even if they did, he convinced himself that the Provisional Government could crush them with ease.

All during the latter part of October, the Military Revolutionary Committee under Soviet Chairman Trotsky's leadership met to discuss strategy and study detailed maps of the city. When at last the final plans were drawn and the last details worked out, the Bolshevik leadership decided that the precise moment to strike had come. All that was needed was an incident to trigger the explosion.

On November 4, 1917, the Military Revolutionary Committee issued a bitterly worded resolution accusing the Provisional Government of undermining the people's liberties. The statement infuriated Kerensky. He decided the time had come to retaliate—to smash the Bolshevik movement with a single well-timed blow.

The following day, Kerensky ordered shock troops, artillery units and army engineers into Petrograd. At five-thirty on the cold and windy morning of November 6, the government troops went into action. Engineers snipped telephone wires to the Smolny Institute, a formerly church-run school where the Bolsheviks had made their headquarters since the March revolution.

In addition to cutting communication lines, the government troops broke into the Bolshevik printing shop. They smashed type, seized documents, officially sealed the doors with wax and posted guards around the building.

When the people of Petrograd awoke that morning they were greeted by a gray, somber sky. Out in the streets everything seemed normal. The streetcars rumbled crankily along, merchants dutifully swept the sidewalks in front of their shops, workers hurried off to their factories.

But to Leon Trotsky, who had just learned that Bolshevik headquarters had been raided, it was not a routine day at all. Lenin was still hiding out in Margarita Fofanova's apartment in the suburbs and could not be reached. Trotsky decided to act on his own. A courier service was quickly organized to maintain communications between the revolutionary leaders in the city. Trotsky ordered a company of the pro-Bolshevik Lithuanian Regiment to escort printers to the printing offices in the Smolny. The government guards surrounding the building offered no resistance when they saw the armed Lithuanians approaching and let them pass. The wax seals on the doors were broken and the printers entered. There was enough undamaged equipment to enable them to print emergency publications.

Trotsky saw that Kerensky's action had played right into Bolshevik hands. It was the chance they had been waiting for. The Bolsheviks had been looking for a way to precipitate the revolution without being cast in the role of instigators. The Provisional Government's raid had provided the ideal opportunity. An uprising now could be justified to the public as a righteous act of self-defense against an aggressive, autocratic government. The move against the Bolsheviks would be depicted as a "counterrevolutionary conspiracy."

Trotsky took pen and paper and drew up a brief decree in the name of the Petrograd Soviet's Military Revolutionary Committee. It was printed and distributed at once to all the troops garrisoned in Petrograd. Many were assumed to be pro-Bolshevik. The decree read: "The enemy of the people took the offensive during the night. The Military Revolutionary Committee is leading the resistance to the assault of the conspirators."

Anticipating retaliatory action by Kerensky, Trotsky and his Committee continued to move quickly. Machine guns and cannon were set up to protect the Smolny against assault. Patrols were posted at the entrances to the gray, three-story building and at nearby street corners. Cartloads of fruit and vegetables were brought to the building in preparation for a long siege. In a matter of hours, the former girls' school had been transformed into an armed fortress.

Evening came. The Smolny was etched sharply against the dancing flames of a dozen bonfires, started by Trotsky's outdoor guards to shield themselves against the freezing cold.

By now, rumors of the Smolny drama were circulating throughout Petrograd and much of Russia. During the night additional military and naval units sent messages to Trotsky declaring that they were coming over to the Bolshevik side. A chain reaction had been set off that could no longer be stopped.

By the next morning the government of Petrograd was virtually in the hands of Trotsky and his Military Revolutionary Committee.

But Kerensky and his fellow ministers were not yet aware of this. They continued to issue orders to regiments in and around the city to put down the uprising. The regimental officers immediately informed Trotsky, who promptly countermanded Kerensky's instructions! It was like a bizarre chess game in which one player is unaware of the pieces he has left, to say nothing of his opponent's moves.

Lenin, still hiding in Margarita Fofanova's apartment, paced the floor like a nervous cat. Having read the morning newspapers he knew that something big had started. Yet the details were so blurred and sparse that he felt completely left out. Moreover, he was hurt that no one had thought to send a messenger to inform him of developments. He sent Mrs. Fofanova to the local Bolshevik headquarters only to discover they were as much in the dark as he.

Lenin had agreed to remain in hiding until his fellow Bolsheviks assured him it was safe to come out in the open. But in view of the new developments he threw caution to the winds. Donning his wig, he left the apartment with a young Finnish revolutionary named Eino Rahja. Around his jaw was a large kerchief that hid his face while making it appear he was suffering from a toothache. Rahja carried two loaded pistols in his pockets for protection.

They hurried down the frozen, wind-swept street and managed to board the last streetcar of the night just as it was clanging shut. They rode in silence toward the Liteiny, one of the numerous bridges across the Neva River which separated the central city of Petrograd from the outlying districts.

Lenin was concerned that they would not be able to cross. He had heard rumors that Kerensky had ordered all the bridges raised in order to cut off the Smolny and the rest of the inner city from outside support.

His fears were groundless. They got off the streetcar, found the Liteiny Bridge down and walked across with no difficulty. Later Lenin was to learn that during the evening Trotsky's forces had quietly captured all ten bridges leading from the working-class quarters to Petrograd itself. A short distance past the bridge, they were startled by the sudden appearance of two mounted cadets from the officers' training corps. This corps was one of the units still loyal to the Provisional Government. Rahja urged Lenin to hurry on. "I'll deal with them," he whispered grimly.

As Lenin melted into the dark, the young Finn began to reel drunkenly. The cadets rode up and demanded his papers. Rahja muttered incoherently that he didn't know what they were talking about. The cadets stared at him in disgust, then wheeled their horses and rode off.

Rahja caught up with Lenin, and soon they reached the Smolny. The icy winds whipping in from the Bay of Finland had cut through to the bone. But the building's warmth quickly renewed their spirits. Although neither Lenin nor Rahja had ever been in the Smolny before, they had no trouble locating Room 100, where the Military Revolutionary Committee was meeting.

Trotsky and the others greeted Lenin with cheerful grins. He was given a full report on all developments. When he asked about the bridges, they informed him that all had been taken. Trotsky added that if things went well, they planned to take control of the entire city without firing a shot!

Lenin could hardly believe his ears. This was not the way revolutions were carried out. He had always assumed the socialist uprising would be accompanied by violence and bloodshed. Yet as he had hurried through the dark Petrograd streets, he had not heard the sound of shooting. Could a successful insurrection really take place so easily?

By morning, Lenin had his answer. During the night there had been several brief skirmishes and a few shots had been exchanged, but there were no casualties. Quietly and stealthily the revolutionaries had occupied the key places in the capital. The government troops seemed to have melted away as soon as the Red Guards appeared. Only two buildings were still in government hands: the huge Winter Palace, where Kerensky and his cabinet were holding out, and the smaller Maryinsky Palace, meeting place of a governmental advisory council. The conquest of Petrograd was virtually complete.

14.

Thunder on the Left

THE PROVISIONAL GOVERNMENT was dead. It had died during the night. But Kerensky and his cabinet did not yet realize it. There were some loyal troops still on the Winter Palace grounds, but these were the only symbol of authority the Provisional Government still retained in Petrograd.

By ten in the morning, Kerensky decided that desperate measures must be taken—fast. Using a private telephone line, he got in touch with the American embassy and asked to borrow an automobile. The vehicle was sent. Kerensky managed to slip out of the palace unnoticed. The car sped him off to the front where he hoped to make contact with the loyal troops and lead them back to the capital.

At about the same time, a small force of Red Guards had marched to the Maryinsky Palace. They broke in on the advisory council meeting there and ordered the members to leave or be arrested. The council dispersed.

Throughout the day Lenin issued statements announcing that the Provisional Government had been overthrown. The distribution of these proclamations was met by a vast public indifference. The streets of Petrograd were strangely silent; there were no cheering throngs of people as the Bolsheviks had hoped. It was almost as if an invisible revolution had taken place.

In the afternoon the members of the Petrograd Soviet met in

the Great Hall of the Smolny. Trotsky got up on the platform and declared in a ringing voice: "So far there hasn't been a single casualty. There cannot be another example in history of a revolutionary movement embracing enormous masses of the population which has taken power so bloodlessly." A thunder of applause greeted his words. No one got up to ask where the "enormous masses" were during the Bolshevik seizure of power.

Lenin was introduced. He spoke briefly of how "the oppressed masses will themselves assume power and shatter the old state apparatus to its foundations." His words received polite, scattered applause. But it was Trotsky's day. To the assembled members of the Bolshevik-controlled Petrograd Soviet he was clearly the hero of the hour.

The following day at two o'clock, the Military Revolutionary Committee ordered troops to the Winter Palace where the Provisional Government was still holding out. They formed a semicircle around the building. Armored cars and field artillery units joined them. A thousand sailors from the nearby naval base at Kronstadt were also moved into the area. A cruiser named the *Aurora* was ordered to anchor in the Neva.

Against this army of 50,000 soldiers, sailors and Red Guards the defending force was minuscule. It consisted of several hundred military cadets, a detachment of Cossacks and a women's battalion of 170 girls in uniform who had had no fighting experience.

Early in the evening, an ultimatum was sent in to the Provisional Government demanding its surrender. The ministers, pinning their hopes on Kerensky's ability to bring back help from the fighting front, rejected the demand and calmly sat down to dinner.

At nine in the evening, the *Aurora* was ordered to fire off a volley of blank shells. Heavy artillery from the Peter and Paul Fortress also discharged rounds of blanks. This set off an exchange of machine gun and small arms fire between the revolutionaries and the Winter Palace defenders. But it was so dark that most of the shots went wild.

The lights in the palace were extinguished. Hour after hour the sporadic shooting went on. At one point the gunners in the Peter and Paul Fortress fired off several rounds of real artillery shells.

These knocked off several cornices and broke some windows in the palace.

In the early hours of the morning, sailors and Red Guards began to infiltrate the royal edifice. In the pitch blackness it was not difficult to do. Most of the Cossacks and women's battalion troops had vanished, leaving only the military cadets to guard the building. Finally, at 2:10 A.M. a revolutionary named Antonov-Ovseyenko burst into a small room where the ministers were sitting. He declared that "in the name of the Military Revolutionary Committee of the Petrograd Soviet" he was placing them under arrest.

News of the Winter Palace's capture spread swiftly to the crowd of soldiers and sailors outside. They forced their way into the building and raced through the corridors and rooms, looting and smashing. Desks and cabinets were ransacked. Some of the looters ripped up expensive leather chairs and tore draperies from the walls in a desperate search for hidden valuables. One Bolshevik official shouted in helpless anger, "Comrades, keep your hands off! That is now the property of the people!"

The looting grew so widespread that armed guards had to be assigned to the building entrances. Pistols drawn, they proceeded to strip everyone of booty as he left the Winter Palace.

The next morning Lenin addressed the Second Congress of Soviets which was meeting at the Smolny. Earlier it had been a scene of unbelievable uproar. The moderates had denounced the Bolsheviks for seizing power in the name of the Petrograd Soviet. Finally, sensing their helplessness to change the course of events, the moderates had simply walked out of the Congress leaving it under the complete control of the Bolsheviks.

A short, stocky figure in shabby trousers that were too long for him, Lenin was hardly an impressive sight. Yet the delegates gave him a thunderous ovation. He waited patiently, his face flushed with victory. Then he said quietly: "We shall now proceed to construct the socialist order."

Lenin spoke of a "just and democratic peace." He called for an immediate armistice that would end the war which had imposed such misery on the working classes. Other speakers followed. But later Lenin rose again to read a "Decree on the Land." It proclaimed the abolition of private ownership of the land, except for land belonging to "simple peasants and simple Cossacks." The peasant delegates cheered and applauded the announcement.

That night a new interim government was established for Russia. It was authorized to rule until the Constituent Assembly, which had been promised by the Provisional Government, could be held. The temporary governing body was to be a council known as the Soviet of People's Commissars. There was no problem in finding a chairman; the obvious choice was Vladimir Lenin. Among the other members were Leon Trotsky, who was to serve as Commissar for Foreign Affairs, and Joseph Stalin, who was named Commissar of Nationalities, a relatively minor office.

Chairman Lenin had barely grown accustomed to his new title before he was faced with his first crisis. Although the Bolsheviks had captured the government, they had not yet won the support and loyalty of the masses. The embittered Mensheviks and other moderates joined forces to establish a Committee of Salvation to oppose the Bolsheviks. The nation was flooded with literature urging the Russian people to ignore the orders of the Bolshevik-controlled soviets. In Petrograd, the Committee of Salvation persuaded civil servants, including postal workers and telegraph operators, to go out on strike. Red Guard patrols were attacked on the streets and in alleys by anti-Bolshevik hit-and-run fighters. And in Moscow there was bitter street fighting between troops of the Bolshevik-dominated Moscow Soviet and military cadets and Cossacks still loyal to the Kerensky government. What's more, Lenin learned to his dismay that Kerensky himself was only twenty miles from the capital, accompanied by a Cossack force commanded by a General Peter Krasnov.

In the crisis, Lenin took over personal control of military operations. His first objective was to establish an armed perimeter around Petrograd to meet the Kerensky threat. Every available piece of artillery was hauled by horse and wagon to the outer defense line. Armor plate and field guns were mounted on railroad cars and engines to help ring the city. Factory delegates were summoned by Lenin, who ordered them to assign every able-bodied worker who could be spared to the defense force. The entire capital was thus mobilized for a last-ditch defense effort. Lenin issued orders tirelessly. There was no detail small enough for him to ignore. However, lack of food and sleep began to tell on him. He grew increasingly irritable and peremptory. No one dared argue with him. Once an order was given it was useless to try to persuade him to countermand it. The slightest hint of a disagreement was enough to drive him into a towering rage.

Trotsky, too, was a dynamo of activity. Working directly with the troops in the field, he visited the ragtag defense army and made rousing speeches. He instructed Red Guards to dig trenches along the perimeter. Troops were stationed at key points and along the routes into the capital.

In a matter of days, Lenin and Trotsky had succeeded in turning Petrograd into a bristling fortress. Meanwhile, the Cossack force accompanying Kerensky was being cleverly infiltrated by Bolshevik agitators. These agents warned General Krasnov's troops that the Petrograd defenders had overwhelming superiority in numbers and arms. The Bolsheviks offered the Cossacks safe-conduct passes if they would desert. By the time Krasnov reached the outskirts of Petrograd, his army had dwindled to a handful. A cold rain enveloped the city. The planned attack on the capital deteriorated into a series of minor skirmishes on the Pulkovo heights overlooking the city. Most of the Cossacks simply threw down their arms and surrendered to the Bolsheviks.

Kerensky began to retreat south, accompanied by a few remaining troops. The pursuing Bolsheviks soon caught up with him, but he managed to slip past a guard and made his escape by automobile, eventually reaching Paris.

In Moscow the Bolsheviks met similar success. Both sides fought desperately, but finally the Red Guards cornered the anti-Bolshevik forces, or White Guards, in the Kremlin, a large complex of government buildings in the heart of the city. Huge guns were trained on the area. The Whites were threatened with immediate annihilation if they did not submit. They surrendered.

In other cities and towns, the Bolsheviks also won control. Determined to crush all opposition, they conducted house-to-house searches in an effort to uncover their enemies. In spite of the pleas of moderates and conservatives for mass resistance, each day saw Lenin's followers increasing and consolidating their control.

In December the people of Russia went to the polls to elect delegates to the promised Constituent Assembly. The vote was a sharp repudiation of the Bolsheviks and their repressive policies. Of 41.7 million votes cast, Lenin's faction received 9.8 million, less than a quarter.

Although many of his associates were shocked, Lenin was not visibly disturbed by the outcome of the election. He had already decided that neither the vote nor a hostile Constituent Assembly would be permitted to stand in his way.

Operating with ruthless efficiency, he ordered the arrest of the entire Electoral Commission. In their place he appointed one of his Bolshevik subordinates, Moses Uritsky, as Commissar of Elections. Uritsky was given full power to examine and pass on the credentials of the elected members of the forthcoming Constituent Assembly. Lenin ordered the closing of the printing presses of the opposition parties. In addition, he replaced the Military Revolutionary Committee with an Extraordinary Commission for Combating Counterrevolution and Sabotage. Better known as the Cheka, the commission was destined to inspire fear in the hearts of millions of Russians. Given unlimited power to root out "enemies of the proletariat," its real function was to terrorize critics of the Bolshevik regime into silence.

On the evening of January 14, Lenin visited a detachment of troops at a military riding school in Petrograd. Afterward, as the automobile in which he was riding slowly pulled away from the building, there was a sudden sharp crackle of gunfire. Three bullets crashed through the windshield, missing him by inches. The attempt at assassination had failed. Nevertheless, for Lenin it was a dramatic and frightening reminder of the terrible burden of personal danger that accompanied dictatorial power.

The Constituent Assembly was to convene in Petrograd at noon on January 18. The day dawned bitterly cold. A heavy sheet of snow covered the capital like a shroud. In many places it piled up in great drifts.

In the late morning, crowds of anti-Bolshevik demonstrators marched toward the Tauride Palace, where the Assembly was to meet. Their banners read "All Power to the Constituent Assembly." Although the paraders were orderly, their mood was one of angry frustration. In two months they had seen most of the freedoms won during the March revolution crushed under the iron fist of the new Bolshevik autocracy.

The Tauride Palace was guarded by a pro-Bolshevik detachment of specially picked sharpshooters. As the demonstrators neared the palace an officer ordered them to halt. They either did not hear the command or refused to obey it. At a distance of less than two hundred feet, the guards raised their weapons and opened fire directly into the crowd. Screams of terror greeted the crackling of the rifles. The marchers scattered in all directions. When the street was cleared, eight or nine men and women were dead and twenty lay wounded in the blood-stained snow. Thus, almost exactly thirteen years after Bloody Sunday of 1905, the slaughter of Father Gapon's followers by the Tsar's troops was reenacted in bizarre fashion.

An hour later a second procession of anti-Bolsheviks approached the Tauride Palace. Once again the troops raised their rifles and fired, killing nearly a dozen demonstrators.

Having terrorized and dispersed the crowds in the streets, the Bolsheviks turned their attention to the deputies inside the meeting hall. By now it had been transformed into an armed camp. Guards with pistols and rifles were stationed at the entrance, supposedly to check credentials. They used the opportunity to insult and intimidate the anti-Bolshevik deputies. Some soldiers talked boisterously of shooting and bayoneting the entire lot of delegates.

For a long while, the meeting hall buzzed with anxious whispers. One man was still absent. Without him nothing could happen. Even the Bolsheviks dared not make a move until he showed up. That man was Lenin.

At two o'clock Lenin, Nadezhda and his sister Maria finally arrived at the Tauride Palace by automobile. A few minutes later, they sat down to tea in a small room off the main meeting hall. In another room nearby, the Bolshevik delegation was holding a noisy caucus. Lenin did not even bother to attend it. He did not have to. Everybody, including Lenin himself, understood that no matter what plans were discussed, it would be his decision that would prevail in the end.

A little before four o'clock Lenin and the Bolshevik deputies entered the assembly hall. The meeting was called to order and the election of a chairman was placed on the floor. The moderates submitted the name of Victor Chernov, Minister of Agriculture in the Kerensky government. The Bolsheviks supported the nomination of a young woman revolutionary named Maria Spiridonova. To their astonishment and dismay, she was decisively defeated by a vote of 244 to 151. Not even the presence of the armed guards throughout the hall had cowed the anti-Bolshevik forces.

When Chernov, the new chairman, arose to deliver his inaugural speech the Bolsheviks jeered and catcalled. They shouted that he was a "Traitor!" and "Counterrevolutionary!" Ignoring them, Chernov made an earnest plea for constitutional democratic government. He argued that only through such a system could Russia be saved. Lenin, seated on the red-carpeted stairs leading to the platform, stretched out and fell asleep, or pretended to do so.

Other speakers got up and denounced the Bolsheviks. One accused them of being "interlopers and wreckers" who did not know the meaning of "creative socialism." Hearing this, an enraged sailor in one of the galleries aimed his rifle at the speaker. A Bolshevik commissar ordered him to put it down. Then a soldier jumped up on the platform and waved a pistol in the speaker's face. There was a shocked gasp from the assembled deputies. Nevertheless, the speaker, a man named Tseretelli, went on as if the soldier were not even there. He made a stirring plea for the delegation of supreme power to the Constituent Assembly on the grounds that it was the people's elected body. The soldier, abashed and uncertain, finally left the platform.

A choice between two programs was placed before the delegates. The Bolshevik proposal called for the establishment of a socialist state in which all power would rest with local and central soviets—or councils—consisting of appointed officials or commissars. Under this system the Constituent Assembly would serve merely to ratify decisions made by the commissars. The moderates, on the other hand, demanded that the elected Constituent Assembly retain fundamental power of government under a constitutional system.

The impatient Bolsheviks now called for the issue to be put to a vote. The balloting was conducted under the eyes of the armed Bolshevik guards. When the votes were counted, Lenin saw that he had suffered another severe defeat. The tally was 237 to 136 in favor of the moderates' proposal for a supreme Constituent Assembly. The Bolsheviks were shaken. They called for a recess and retired to discuss their next move. They were gone only a short time. When they returned to the hall it was to announce that they were withdrawing from the Constituent Assembly!

Just before leaving the Tauride Palace, Lenin turned to a young sailor named Zheleznikov who was in charge of the guard and gave him his instructions. Once the session ended, Lenin told him, the delegates were to be dispersed. No one was to be permitted to return to the palace the next day. There were to be no more sessions of the Constituent Assembly!

The meeting went on into the early morning hours. The moderate delegates stubbornly continued to ignore the jeering and threats from the soldiers and sailors in the balcony. They passed a number of items of legislation to implement their program. Finally, at four thirty in the morning the sailor Zheleznikov marched up the carpeted steps to the platform and tapped Chairman Chernov on the shoulder. "You must finish now," he announced. "I have orders from the People's Commissar."

Chernov was incredulous. "What People's Commissar?" he demanded.

The sailor shrugged. "You can't stay. The guards are tired. We will turn out the lights."

The angry chairman turned away from Zheleznikov and tried to continue the meeting. The soldiers and sailors began to shout at Chernov and the other deputies: "Enough of this! Get out of here!"

A minute later the lights were turned out. The deputies stumbled around in the dark, fearful of being shot as they left the palace. Eventually they made their way to the main entrance. Contrary to their expectations, the guards did not molest them as they left. A heavy mist blanketed the city streets as they departed into the night.

The curtailed Constituent Assembly had sat for a total of only thirteen hours. Across the nation, people reacted with shock and anger. Even within the Bolshevik-dominated soviets, pointed questions were directed at Lenin. Why had he dissolved the Assembly? Who was responsible for ordering soldiers to shoot down men and women in an unarmed procession?

Lenin sought to argue that "the people" felt there was no room in Russia's new socialist system for a Constituent Assembly. After all, it was merely a vestige of the bourgeois Kerensky government. "We called the Assembly only because the people wanted us to convoke it," Lenin pointed out. "But the people soon realized what it really represents, and therefore we are fulfilling the will of the people who had declared, "All power to the Soviets!'"

As for the violence against the marchers, that was unavoidable— a natural outgrowth of revolution. "We cannot present a socialist revolution to the people in a clear-cut, pristine and flawless form," he asserted.

The evasive explanation did not satisfy the critics. Lenin himself began to sense that he had made a grave mistake in handling the Constituent Assembly issue as he had. At first he tried to convince himself that the dissolution of the Constituent Assembly at least served to symbolize the formal liquidation of bourgeois democracy in Russia. But afterward he admitted to Trotsky that it would have been better to postpone the Assembly indefinitely rather than summarily disperse it.

As criticism mounted, Lenin stepped up his efforts to safeguard his position of power. His major concern was the "enemies of the regime." The Cheka redoubled its efforts to root out "traitors" and "bourgeois bootlickers." Hundreds were quietly arrested, often at night, and thrown into prison. The civil liberties guaranteed by the Provisional Government were discarded.

On one occasion, two ill former ministers of the Kerensky government were murdered in a hospital by two sailors who decided that the former officials were "counterrevolutionaries." A committee of investigation under the Commissar of Justice interrogated witnesses, reconstructed the crime and learned the names of the murderers. But at a meeting of the Soviet of People's Commissars, Lenin refused to authorize the arrest of the sailors. Several of the commissars were aghast. They argued that if murderers could get away scot-free, there was no telling where it would end. But Lenin was adamant. "I don't really feel the people are interested in such matters," he retorted blandly. "After all, how many workers or peasants have ever heard of these dead ministers?"

Another immediate challenge facing Lenin and his Bolsheviks was ending the war. Peace had been a key issue in his campaign against the Kerensky government. In December, soon after gaining power, Lenin had sent Trotsky, as Commissar for Foreign Affairs, to Brest-Litovsk near the Polish border to arrange a settlement with the Germans. Germany agreed to a temporary truce while a permanent peace was negotiated. But her demands were so exorbitant that the talks stalled. The Germans insisted that Russian territory already occupied by their armies be kept by Germany. This included Poland, Estonia, Latvia, Lithuania and vast areas of the Ukraine. In all, Russia stood to lose a third of her farm land, half of her industrial facilities and almost all of her iron and coal resources. Furthermore, Germany was demanding an indemnity of three billion rubles!

Trotsky decided that such a settlement would ruin Russia. He advised Lenin against accepting such outrageous terms. But Lenin was less concerned with a loss of territory than with endangering his revolution. "And what if we refuse to accept the Germans' peace terms and they attack," he demanded of Trotsky. "What then?"

"We would then sign the peace terms," Trotsky replied, "but only under the threat of German bayonets. At least the working masses throughout the world would know why we were accepting such impossible demands."

Lenin was far from convinced. He was for peace at any price. He reasoned that after the war there would be a socialist revolution in Germany anyway; and in such an event Russia would not be required to give up any territory or pay indemnities to a sister socialist nation.

A large-scale debate over the peace issue took place within Bolshevik circles. Lenin's proposal for immediate acceptance of Germany's terms was rejected by the majority of the leaders in favor of Trotsky's recommendation.

On February 10, Trotsky returned to Brest-Litovsk to meet again with the Germans. He astounded them by announcing that Russia was withdrawing from the war without signing a peace treaty.

"We are issuing orders for the full demobilization of troops now confronting the armies of Germany, Austria-Hungary, Turkey and Bulgaria," he told them. But he protested that Russia could not sign a peace treaty with conditions that would carry "oppression, sorrow and suffering to millions of human beings."

The German representative, General Hoffmann, was so taken aback that he could only mutter that the Bolshevik action was "unheard of." When Hoffmann's report reached his superiors in Berlin they were just as amazed. Russia's action was unprecedented in the history of diplomacy.

For the next six days Germany hesitated, not quite sure how to meet the situation. Finally she announced that unless Russia accepted her peace terms at once, she would renew hostilities on February 18.

In Petrograd the foreign policy debate was renewed as a result of the German decision. Lenin was more certain than ever that Trotsky's strategy was wrong. Now, he felt, there was no choice but to accept the German terms immediately.

Events seemed to strengthen his hand. On February 18, the Germans launched a lightning offensive. Within five days they knifed 150 miles deeper into Russia, capturing vast stores of ammunition. Only a miracle could prevent them from plunging on to Petrograd itself. Anticipating the danger, Lenin decided to move the capital to Moscow. But capitulation was now inevitable. Faced with the threat of annihilation, the Bolsheviks agreed to surrender. On March 3, 1918, Russia and Germany signed the Treaty of Brest-Litovsk, based on the harsh German terms. It was ratified two weeks later at the All-Russian Congress of Soviets in Moscow.

The treaty was greeted with angry denunciation from one end of Russia to the other. It was termed a "shameful treaty." Many socialists accused Lenin of betraying the international revolutionary movement in accepting a peace imposed by the German imperialists. But he defended himself vigorously. Was it not better to give up a third of Russia than risk losing the revolution in Russia? he demanded.

Although he found himself in the eye of a storm of controversy, Lenin moved ahead determinedly with his Bolshevik program. In this way he hoped not only to consolidate his power but to divert public attention from the Brest-Litovsk Treaty. He forced through laws providing for the drafting of workers by the government. The inheritance of private property was outlawed. Another decree substituted the Gregorian calendar, common throughout the Western world, for the old Julian calendar, which had been two weeks behind the Gregorian. Moreover, to reinforce the growing separation of the Bolsheviks from the Mensheviks and other Social Democrats, Lenin announced that hereafter the Bolsheviks would be known as the *Communist Party*.

Yet in spite of Lenin's efforts to stifle dissent, opposition to his regime grew rather than subsided. In addition to civilian dissatisfaction, there was now a new and growing military threat. Peace with Germany had freed hundreds of thousands of Russian troops from the battlefield. Among them were many who were ready to fight to free Russia from the iron fist of the new Communist dictatorship. At the same time, Russia's former allies, still involved in war, were angered by the separate peace she had signed with Germany. They felt Russia had betrayed the Allied cause. Furthermore, Communism with its advocacy of worldwide revolution appeared to many to threaten the very fabric of Western civilization. Government leaders in the United States, Great Britain and France decided that the Leninist regime must be toppled.

By the summer of 1918 anti-Communist Russian units, supported by supplies, money and men from the Allied nations, had formed in all corners of Russia. Calling themselves the White armies, they penetrated deep into Communist-held territory from every direction. To Lenin the danger of losing his revolution seemed more imminent than at any time since he had seized power eight months earlier.

15.

The Red Terror

As THE WHITE ARMIES advanced, they were aided by acts of subversion and terror from within the Communist-controlled areas. Murders and sabotage by anti-Bolsheviks were commonplace. In one instance the German ambassador, Count Mirbach, was assassinated by the Social Revolutionaries, radical rivals of the Bolsheviks. The killing was designed to embarrass the fledgling Red government. In order to combat such acts and stifle opposition Lenin ordered the Cheka to step up its efforts.

The Cheka's agents went to work with a ruthless efficiency that put the old tsarist police to shame. A reign of terror was launched that resulted in the deaths of hundreds of thousands of Russians. In some districts martial law was declared. Men and women were arrested and imprisoned or even put to death without hearings or a trial.

In the White-held sectors similar practices were widespread. Among the ex-tsarist officers, Cossacks and anti-Communist radicals who made up the White forces there were many adventurers and even former criminals. They saw the civil war as an opportunity to win money and power. Some of the Whites were viciously cruel men who found pleasure in torture and murder. They thought nothing of razing entire villages and killing every inhabitant they could find. It was a tragic moment, a time when Russian soil was stained with blood that would leave its mark for decades to come.

THE RED TERROR 163

As the Whites continued their steady advance Lenin's sense of desperation grew. A vexing problem was the presence of the Tsar and his family, whom the Communists had inherited from the Kerensky government. The Romanovs were in custody in Sverdlovsk, western Siberia. As long as Nicholas II lived, he served as a dangerous symbol of prerevolutionary Russia, a figure behind whom many Whites could rally.

Lenin made a swift and coldly calculated decision.

On the night of July 16, 1918, soldiers of the detail assigned to guard the royal family tramped up the stairs of the house in Sverdlovsk and awakened them. The former Tsar, his wife Alix, their children, their servants and the family physician were urged to dress quickly. Nicholas demanded to know why. He was told by the officer in charge that there might be trouble and it was important to get the family to a safer place. Was there time for tea? Nicholas asked. Yes, he was told, provided they did not dally.

After tea, the prisoners were led downstairs to a room where chairs had been lined up along a single wall. The guards ordered them to sit down. It was a strange command, but they did as they were told. A paper was handed to Nicholas. It was a death warrant —for the entire Romanov family! The warrant had been issued by the local soviet.

There was barely time for the terrible significance of the order to sink in before a guard drew a revolver and pointed it directly at Nicholas. Horrified, the former ruler threw out his hands to protect his thirteen-year-old son. At that precise moment the pistol discharged and a bullet exploded in his face. He slumped to the floor. It was a signal for the other guards to raise their guns and fire furiously at the helpless prisoners. The screams of dying adults and children mingled with the angry roar of rifles. The little dog of one of Nicholas' daughters yelped in terror. A guard took careful aim and shot it dead. Now the soldiers began to use their bayonets and the butt ends of their rifles to make sure the job was completed.

In a few moments it was all over. The floor was covered with dead bodies awash in a great pool of blood. The entire royal family was gone, victims of the horrible mass slaughter. Also dead were their personal servants, physician and pet dog. All the living tsarist symbols which Lenin had feared and hated had fallen beneath the hail of Red bullets. And with their passing had gone the last vestiges of restraint shown by the Communist regime.

Lenin did his best to keep the details of the murders from becoming public. But little by little, the full story got out. Surprisingly, it created little stir in a nation torn by bloody civil war. As the White armies continued their forward thrust, the Red forces, now under the command of Trotsky, retreated. In their wake the opposing armies left whole areas of Russia in misery, famine and desolation.

On the morning of August 30, Moses Uritsky, chairman of the hated Cheka, was shot to death by a young intellectual while leaving his office. The news sent chills down the spines of many Bolshevik leaders. Some were convinced the Uritsky killing was the signal for a mass uprising. They warned Lenin not to make any public appearances. Although shaken by the assassination, he stubbornly insisted that he had no intention of breaking his schedule. Nadezhda, who might have restrained him, was away at a meeting.

That evening, Lenin was driven by his burly chauffeur-bodyguard, Stepan Gil, to a workers' assembly in the Basmannaya district northwest of the Kremlin. After speaking for an hour, he and Gil drove to a meeting of a factory committee where he launched a bitter attack on "forces of reaction," particularly the United States of America. Outside the factory building Gil waited patiently behind the wheel of the car for Lenin to come out. A hatless young woman, clutching a dark handbag, approached the car and quietly asked whether Lenin had arrived. Gil, under instructions to reveal nothing, parried the question by replying that he knew nothing about the speakers inside. The woman shrugged and entered the factory.

Some time later Lenin emerged, flanked by a group of excited admirers. As they approached the car, a shot rang out. Gil whirled around in his seat. He glimpsed the hatless woman standing close to Lenin and holding a smoking revolver. Before he could move, she fired two more shots. Lenin slumped to the ground. The chauffeur reached for his own pistol and leaped out of the automobile. By now the woman had started to run. Gil aimed at her head, but refrained from pulling the trigger because of the crowd.

He turned instead to his fallen superior and knelt beside him to see if he was alive. Lenin was still breathing.

Several workers helped Gil place the wounded man in the back seat of the automobile. Jamming the accelerator to the ground, the chauffeur raced back to Lenin's house in the Kremlin compound. A doctor was called. Then a car was dispatched to fetch Nadezhda.

When she arrived, almost hysterical, she found the house crowded with strangers. Gil tried to reassure her that her husband was only "slightly wounded." Nevertheless she gasped and rushed upstairs to the bedroom. Lenin lay on the bed, deathly pale, surrounded by half a dozen doctors. "You must be tired," he murmured to Nadezhda in a small strained voice. "Go and lie down."

Two of the three bullets fired had struck Lenin. One had pierced his lung and lodged in the neck; the other was imbedded in his shoulder. For the next week and a half, he hovered between life and death. But he fought for life stubbornly. Several times a day medical bulletins were issued on his condition. Finally, at the end of ten days, his pulse and temperature subsided. It was evident that he would pull through. However, the doctors warned that the bullets could not be removed and he would carry them in him for the rest of his days.

The assassination of Uritsky and the attempt on Lenin's life set off a new reign of official terror. During the months that followed, the Petrograd Cheka rounded up and summarily executed more than eight hundred "enemies of the people." In other cities, the local Chekas followed similar policies.

Meanwhile the woman who had shot Lenin had been quickly identified and arrested. She was Fanya Kaplan, a thirty-five-year-old Social Revolutionary, who was convinced Lenin had betrayed the revolution by dissolving the Constituent Assembly. Accordingly, she had decided that he must be removed in order to save Russia.

Fanya Kaplan was imprisoned in a basement room of the Kremlin and questioned mercilessly by Cheka agents. She stubbornly refused to say where she had obtained the gun or who her accomplices were, if any. Finally, when the Cheka was convinced it could get nothing more out of her, its leaders ordered her killed. A young sailor named Pavel Malkov, assigned to duty as the commandant of the Kremlin, was given the job of executioner. On September 3 he dutifully went down to the room where she was being held, quickly drew out his pistol and shot her through the back of the head.

Within a week after the doctors announced that he was out of danger, Lenin was sitting up in bed. He insisted on getting reports from the fighting fronts—only to learn that the Whites were continuing to overrun Red territory; Communist forces were pulling back in every sector. With the nation wracked by civil war, there was famine and misery everywhere. All goods and services were in short supply. Power failures were a daily occurrence. Conditions were even worse now than during the bleakest days under the Tsar or Kerensky.

Finally, in mid-September, the picture began to brighten. In southern Russia, the Red army won a striking victory. Led by Trotsky, the troops had defeated a large force of White Guards at Kazan, then raced on to capture Simbirsk, the town of Lenin's birth. Just as important as the military implications of the victory was its psychological significance. As the first major triumph for the Communists it helped rally greater support from the masses. Indeed, it was to prove to be the turning point of the war. Lenin sent a telegram of congratulations to Trotsky, urging him on to even greater efforts.

The success at Kazan seemed to speed Lenin's recovery. Within a week of the victory he was out of bed and presiding over meetings of the Communist Party's Central Committee. The fingers of his left hand were still stiff, but he was in high spirits.

Nevertheless, the doctors warned that he must not overtax himself and insisted that he take a brief vacation. Under the prodding of Nadezhda and his sister Maria he finally agreed. They went to a spacious country house on an estate at Gorki twenty miles from Moscow. There, away from the hubbub of the Kremlin, they tried to rest and relax. For once, Nadezhda had a chance to be alone with her husband and to talk with him. But, characteristically, he insisted on discussing politics. Nadezhda noted unhappily that he had changed during the months he had been in power. His outlook seemed harder and colder than before. She was shocked when he spoke almost matter-of-factly of a group of Mensheviks who had been condemned to death as "counterrevolutionaries." When she questioned the need of such a cruel policy, he replied bluntly: "If we don't shoot a few of the leaders opposed to us now, we may have to shoot ten thousand workers who will follow them, later on."

Nadezhda did not share his cold-blooded approach to the taking of human life. She was particularly distressed by the shooting of Fanya Kaplan and mentioned this to Lenin. The thought of a revolutionary government executing a young woman revolutionary—no matter how misguided she may have been—seemed unconscionable to Nadezhda. She was so affected that while talking with Lenin about it she began to cry. Lenin replied that he too regretted the killing of his would-be assassin but that it was an unfortunate necessity.

For the rest of 1918 and all through 1919, Lenin was beset by a host of difficulties. Although the Red armies were now on the offensive and advancing steadily, it was bloody work. The final defeat of Germany in November 1918 brought the World War to an end. Some troops of the Western allies were reassigned to Russia to aid the White armies. A blockade was instituted against Communist Russia, thus intensifying the nation's economic woes. And early in 1919 a new calamity was added to the burdens of the Russian people—typhus! A deadly disease whose symptom was abnormally high fever, it soon spread to epidemic proportions. Daily, Russians, weakened by deprivation and cold, toppled over in the streets. In Moscow alone, typhus claimed thousands of victims. The bodies had to be stacked up in the cemeteries like cordwood to await the spring when the ground would be soft enough to bury them.

Lenin now recognized how far-fetched his simplistic prerevolutionary notion of government had been. Engels had predicted that after the socialist revolution the state would become unnecessary and would wither away. Lenin had accepted this concept in principle. He had even boasted that any worker could be transformed into a government minister in a few days. But once having shouldered the burden of rule, he suddenly had discovered to his dismay that in a highly developed society the role of government is a complex one. Decisions, he learned, had to be based on a diversity of social, economic and political considerations. He found, furthermore, that in the absence of trained administrators and engineers, Marxist dogma alone was powerless to keep railroad trains running on schedule or power stations from breaking down.

In truth, economic activity in Russia had come to a virtual standstill. Famine, disease and war paralyzed the nation. Factories were operating at a fraction of capacity. There was a severe shortage of skilled personnel to man the industrial complex which had been taken over by the Communist government. Hundreds of thousands of the bourgeoisie, which included the managerial and professional classes, were emigrating from Russia. True, under the new laws promulgated by Lenin, anyone could be drafted to work for the government. But not even the force of law could guarantee that an anti-Bolshevik factory manager or production engineer would not sabotage industrial operations.

The production of goods and services continued to fall off. In dismay, Lenin ordered thousands of administrators, technicians and skilled workers suspected of "economic sabotage" arrested. Hundreds were shot. But this only intensified the shortage of qualified manpower and increased the nation's industrial problems.

Throughout the year 1920 Lenin and his fellow commissars tried desperately to shore up the crumbling economy along Communist principles. Yet nothing seemed to work out as Marx and Engels had predicted. With the elimination of private ownership, incentive seemed to have disappeared. In the factories where committees of workers were set up to help establish basic policy, conditions were chaotic.

Report after report reached Lenin's desk indicating the apparent failure of Communist programs. A nagging sense of doubt and uncertainty began to plague him. Perhaps they had gone too far, too fast. He wondered whether there had been enough time for the masses to understand and accept socialism. Defensively, he began to castigate everyone—the peasants, rival radical factions, the White Guard, foreign interventionists. But he carefully avoided accepting any personal responsibility for Russia's plight.

For three years Lenin had wielded dictatorial powers. No member of his regime dared to dispute his authority. He had ruled virtually by edict, making all the final decisions himself. Yet if he experienced a sense of guilt over the initial failure of Marxism, he never hinted at it publicly.

At the end of February 1921, Lenin addressed the Moscow Soviet. To the amazement of most of the members present, he proposed a radical departure from traditional socialist concepts. He called for a New Economic Policy, a program that would combine socialism with some features of capitalism! Farmers would be allowed to sell surplus grain on the open market for a profit instead of surrendering it to the state. Small industries would be leased to private ownership. A modified wage system would be reintroduced to give people an economic incentive to work harder.

Although the changes were modest, they represented a revolutionary compromise with the fundamental tenets of Marxism. Many of the old-line revolutionaries muttered bitterly about the betrayal of socialist ideals. But few dared to voice open criticism. Anticipating opposition, Lenin had given orders to the Cheka to deal with the slightest breach of political discipline "strictly, severely and mercilessly."

For the Russian masses, however, the New Economic Policy had immense psychological effects. Almost overnight, the entire national economy seemed to be roused out of its lethargy. Industrial production started to climb. The morale of workers and peasants began to improve.

The outlook grew even brighter with the signing of peace treaties with the interventionist governments providing for the withdrawal of their troops from Russian soil. It meant that seven years of continuous warfare had come to an end.

Suddenly, in the spring of 1921, the nation's modest recovery began to grind to a halt. Famine, the eternal foe, descended like a plague. Droughts, dust storms and swarms of locusts joined together to ruin the harvest in the rich farming lands along the Volga. It was the most critical famine in thirty years. Starving peasants abandoned their farms to seek relief in the overcrowded cities which had neither food nor facilities to feed or house them. Men, women and children died by the millions.

Reluctantly, Lenin allowed International Red Cross and American relief organizations to enter Russia to feed the suffering peasants. But he was chagrined to have to admit to his own people and the world that he needed the help of capitalist countries. He also feared that the Russians would be contaminated by bourgeois propaganda and contacts with foreigners. Consequently he gave orders that only the children were to be fed! But it was impossible for even the ruthlessly efficient Cheka to enforce such an impractical decree; before long the Americans were secretly passing out food to the hungry grownups as well.

In addition to the continuing political crises, Lenin found himself beset by personal problems as well. Early in 1922 he began to suffer severe headaches and spells of dizziness. The prospect of being incapacitated when he was needed most troubled him greatly. Poor health also intensified his frustration with the mountain of obstacles that refused to disappear. The army of Communist bureaucrats—many of them incompetent—had grown to massive proportions. The government officials were taking on all the attributes of a new privileged class. The situation made a mockery of the original Marxist concepts. For Lenin the final irony was the fact that the one program that had given promise of success was the New Economic Policy with its reintroduction of capitalistic techniques!

16.

Death of a Revolutionary

IN MARCH 1922, Lenin attended the Eleventh Congress of the Communist Party. He was drawn and white; recurring attacks of pain drove him nearly frantic. Nevertheless, he managed to control the Congress with his customary iron grip. Addressing the delegates, he denounced some of the inadequacies and stupidities of the governmental bureaucracy and demanded immediate reforms. As a means of improving efficiency and discipline he recommended the creation of the post of General Secretary to the Central Committee of the Communist Party. The man he chose for the job was Joseph Stalin. Until now Stalin had held relatively minor posts such as Commissar of Nationalities. But he had impressed Lenin. Although not brilliant, he was ambitious, hard-working and efficient. Lenin felt Stalin's talents were just what was needed to improve operation of the creaking Party machinery.

At the same time, the ailing Lenin knew that he himself might not be able to continue for long as head of the Soviet of People's Commissars. Who could succeed him? He had thought a great deal about it, and in the end he could think of only one man, Leon Trotsky. Trotsky alone, he decided, had the creative imagination and razor-sharp intellect to bring the nation through the crises that loomed ahead.

Lenin offered him the post of deputy chairman of the Soviet, thereby establishing him as his heir-apparent. To his surprise, Trotsky turned it down! Although not a modest man, Trotsky felt that his talents did not match Lenin's. He also feared that by accepting such a role now, he would give the impression of *wanting* to replace Lenin, thus provoking jealousy and resentment. Moreover, he and Stalin did not get along, and he was worried lest personal conflict between two of Lenin's appointees would split the Party. Lenin was disappointed, but he accepted Trotsky's refusal with good grace, fully aware of the reasons behind it.

One morning toward the end of May, Dr. Rozanov, one of Lenin's physicians, was hastily summoned to the house at Gorki. He found Nadezhda and Lenin's sister Maria frantic with worry. They reported that during the night Lenin had suffered intense stomach pains and headaches. In addition, his speech was slurred and his right side was partially paralyzed.

The physician guessed at once that Lenin had suffered a stroke, with probable brain damage. He ordered his patient to bed immediately. For the next three weeks, Lenin was immobilized. His wife and sister kept him to a strict schedule. Then he began to recover his strength. Chafing under the restrictions, he insisted on receiving visitors. With the physician's approval, Nadezhda and Maria relented. One of the most frequent visitors was Joseph Stalin. He reported on political developments, but he said very little about his own activities as General Secretary of the Party.

By fall Lenin was able to return to Moscow to resume a restricted work schedule in the Kremlin. He was surprised and disturbed by some of the things that had taken place during his absence. Stalin, he found, had quietly managed to concentrate considerable political power in his own hands. As General Secretary, he had set up a control network by replacing many of the local Party secretaries with appointees loyal to himself and intimidating and arresting his opponents.

In mid-December, Lenin's stomach pains and headaches returned and he began vomiting. The doctors found that he had suffered a second stroke and again ordered him to bed. While sensing the seriousness of his condition, Lenin nevertheless protested that he had important work to do. With Stalin engaged in an obvious drive for power, he decided that any delay in meeting the threat might be disastrous. Indeed, Lenin was so agitated that the physicians reluctantly gave him permission to work with a secretary. They feared that denying him this privilege might be even worse for his physical condition.

Over the next several days the bedridden Lenin painfully dictated an important statement. He was so enfeebled that he could work for only short periods at a time. Uppermost in his mind was the future of the world's first Communist government. Having seen the power Stalin had already accumulated in his brief absence, he dreaded to think what would happen after he was gone.

The statement was a kind of political "last will and testament." It addressed itself to the Communist leadership, stressing the need for a change in the Party's political organization. The statement called for a drastic enlargement of the Communist Central Committee to provide for wider representation of the working class. For Lenin this represented a surprising change of outlook. The experience of the past four years had convinced him that while a small elite group might be necessary to lead a revolution, it could not effectively rule a nation. Political stability required that the masses themselves be given a greater role in government.

The statement went on to discuss the matter of Lenin's own successor, thus touching on the most explosive issue of all. Lenin sensed that the two leading contenders were Stalin and Trotsky. For some time he had recognized a growing enmity between them. If a clash over the succession took place after he was gone it could split the Party and all of Russia.

There was no question in his mind that Trotsky was the logical heir. He admired Trotsky's intelligence and selfless dedication, just as he now viewed the overly ambitious Stalin with resentment and distrust. He was troubled not only by Stalin's ruthless bid for more power, but by his growing reputation for needless violence. In fact, at that very moment Stalin was engaged in a drive to bring his own native Georgia into closer harmony with the rest of Soviet Russia through brute force. Thousands of vicious beatings and murders marked the course of the campaign to win the Georgians over to Communism.

Lenin reflected his thorough disenchantment with Stalin by dictating the following:

> Comrade Stalin, having become General Secretary, has concentrated immeasurable power in his hands, and I am not sure that he always knows how to use that power with sufficient caution. On the other hand Comrade Trotsky . . . is distinguished not only by his exceptional abilities—personally, to be sure, he is perhaps the most able man on the present C.C. [Central Committee]—but also by his excessive self-assurance and excessive enthusiasm for the purely administrative aspect of his work.
>
> These two qualities of the two most eminent leaders of the present C.C. might, quite innocently, lead to a split, and if our party does not take steps to prevent it, a split might arise unexpectedly.

It was a remarkable document. Lenin was asking that the base of the government be broadened so that eventually the dictatorship could be liquidated. At the same time, he was making it clear that his own choice of successor was Leon Trotsky.

Having thus dealt with the two issues that troubled him the most, he instructed the secretary to type up five copies. Under no circumstances must their existence be made known to anyone, he told her. She understood. One copy was to remain with him, three were to be kept by Nadezhda and the fifth was to go into a secret file in his office in the Kremlin. On the envelope of the copies for Nadezhda, he instructed the girl to write: "To be opened only by V. I. Lenin or in the event of his death by Nadezhda Konstantinovna."

As the days passed, Lenin's condition remained unchanged. Except for the secretaries and his immediate family he was forbidden visitors. His sole contact with political developments outside his room was through Nadezhda and his sister Maria. While all Russia waited anxiously for news of the famous patient, Lenin himself was in a curiously mild and detached frame of mind. From time to time he dictated additional brief statements to his secretaries. These reflected an extension of the change in thinking that had gone into his "last testament." Perhaps realization of the seriousness of his condition had instilled a gentler, more humanistic outlook. Gone was much of the old fanaticism that had characterized the professional revolutionary.

Lenin now seemed to feel that Marx's dream of a socialist utopia had been distorted into a ruthless, oppressive dictatorship. The autocracy of the Tsar had been replaced by a Communist absolutism that represented for the people of Russia little real change in their way of life. In its single-minded determination to take and retain power, the Communist Party had committed endless crimes against the masses. And Lenin felt that he himself was most of all to blame, for he had led the revolution. Only by giving the government back to the workers and peasants could the nation be saved. . . .

At the end of December, Lenin learned from Nadezhda and his sister Maria about additional atrocities committed against the people of Georgia by Stalin and several of his associates. The news infuriated him. He denounced Stalin and two other officials named Ordjonikidze and Dzerzhinsky, calling them "typical Russian bureaucrats, rascals and lovers of violence." Then, gripped by a sense of personal anguish and guilt, he called for a secretary and dictated a brief statement for his private files: "I am, I believe, strongly guilty before the workers of Russia for not having intervened energetically or drastically enough . . . we have taken over from Tsarism [the same Russian apparatus], only tarring it a little with the Soviet brush."

Bitterly, Lenin had to acknowledge that of all his mistakes the worst had been the appointment of Stalin to a position where he could amass great power. He now dictated several additional paragraphs, instructing the secretary to add them as a kind of postscript to his political "last testament." The statement read in part as follows:

> Stalin is too coarse, and this fault, though tolerable in dealing among us Communists, becomes unbearable in a General Secretary. Therefore I propose to the comrades to find some way of removing Stalin from his position and appointing somebody else who differs in all respects from Comrade Stalin

in one characteristic—namely, someone more tolerant, more loyal, more polite and considerate. . . .

Lenin's anxiety about Stalin continued unabated. He lay in bed and brooded silently. Isolated as he was in his sickbed, he could do almost nothing to oppose Stalin in person. Yet it was clear the Georgian meant to usurp dictatorial power as soon as possible, using any means necessary. Finally, completely frustrated by his own sense of helplessness, Lenin called in Nadezhda and dictated a brief message to Stalin. He reproved the General Secretary in the severest possible terms and warned that he would oppose him in his efforts to seize power.

Nadezhda sent the note to Stalin by messenger. Shortly afterward, she received an outraged phone call from the General Secretary. He was so rude and vulgar that she thought at first he must be drunk. Stalin obviously was convinced that Nadezhda had inspired the message from Lenin. He reviled her and accused her of blackening his name before her husband. She had no right to discuss Party matters about which she knew nothing, he shouted angrily. Then he adopted a threatening tone and warned that she had better take care not to damage the Party further.

Nadezhda was reduced to tears and hysterics. Stalin had insulted and frightened her, but nevertheless she did not want to tell Lenin and worry him. In desperation, she turned to her husband's longtime supporter Kamenev and related what had happened. Kamenev rushed to Stalin and angrily demanded an explanation for his atrocious behavior. But the wily General Secretary calmed Kamenev down and talked confidingly to him. In the end, he managed to persuade Kamenev to become a member of a conspiracy to set up a three-man dictatorship after Lenin died! The triumvirate was to consist of Stalin himself, Grigory Zinoviev and Kamenev.

For two and a half months, while his physical condition worsened steadily, Lenin remained ignorant of the telephone conversation between Stalin and Nadezhda. However, word of the General Secretary's boorish behavior toward his wife finally reached him. He was infuriated. Weak as he was, he managed to dictate the following letter to Stalin, with copies for Kamenev and Zinoviev:

Dear Comrade Stalin!

You permitted yourself a rude summons of my wife to the telephone and you went on to reprimand her rudely. . . . I have no intention of forgetting so easily something which has been done against me, and I do not have to stress that I consider anything done against my wife as done against me. I am therefore asking you to weigh carefully whether you agree to retract your words and apologize, or whether you prefer the severance of relations between us.

Sincerely,
Lenin

Stalin knew he was on the horns of a dilemma as soon as he received Lenin's note. If he refused to apologize, he would be attacked by his enemies for having insulted the wife of the world's leading Communist. On the other hand, if he sent a letter of apology it was tantamount to an admission of serious error. Either way, he stood to lose.

Stalin delayed his decision as long as possible. Having learned through private Kremlin sources that Lenin's condition had deteriorated, he apparently hoped that Lenin would be dead before it became necessary for him to apologize. However, through sheer willpower, Lenin managed to hang on to life.

By March 7, Stalin felt he could delay no longer. Weighing the two alternatives, he decided a letter of apology was far less of a risk than ignoring the demand for a retraction. Even bedridden, Lenin could be a formidable foe because of his stature among the Communist leadership.

Stalin wrote the apology to Nadezhda. She read it with mild satisfaction. But Lenin was not content. He had made up his mind that Stalin must go, and in the interests of the Russian people he was prepared to devote his final hours to this end. Accordingly, he instructed his secretaries to get from the files all relevant documents referring to Stalin's role in the Georgian atrocities. When the reports and correspondence were collected, he ordered them placed in Trotsky's hands. Along with the documents, he sent a message asking Trotsky to use them to expose Stalin at the Twelfth Communist Party Congress to be held the following month.

Trotsky hesitated. He felt uncertain of his ability to handle Stalin singlehanded. Lenin had indicated he would not be satisfied with anything less than expulsion of the General Secretary and his henchmen from their posts. Trotsky was convinced such an objective would be difficult if not impossible to achieve. Why not a simple reprimand on condition that they mend their ways in the future? he suggested.

Lenin was dismayed by Trotsky's equivocal reply. He was certain that aside from himself Trotsky was the only other man in the Party capable of influencing the delegates to the Party Congress to get rid of Stalin. Yet here was Trotsky clearly afraid to undertake the battle, trying to persuade himself that Stalin might be prevailed upon to change his policies. Could the tiger be expected to change his stripes?

Wearily, Lenin informed Lydia Fotieva, the secretary who had been serving as his emissary to Trotsky, not to press the issue further. He knew Trotsky too well to think that further argument could get him to change his mind.

Two days later Lenin suffered his third stroke.

The attack left his right side completely paralyzed and partially affected his left side. It robbed him of the power of speech. In addition, he began to run a high fever. From the sickroom at Gorki the doctors issued medical bulletins that gave the impression Lenin was recovering. But privately they conceded that he would be dead in a few hours or days.

Yet Lenin managed to hang on somehow. For the next two months he hovered between life and death. Then, miraculously, he began to improve. By midsummer the paralysis disappeared from his left side, although his right side remained completely immobilized. The color returned to his cheeks and he seemed well on his way to recovery. Nadezhda gave him daily lessons to teach him to speak. He started to walk again, using a cane and dragging his right leg. One day in September, he amazed his physicians by walking down a flight of stairs alone, holding on to the banister. He began to read newspapers and started teaching himself to write with his left hand.

Each day, too, he went outdoors to gather mushrooms or for a motorcar ride with his chauffeur, Stepan Gil. These were quiet, pleasant days. Lenin, occupied with the simplicities of life, was constantly relaxed and in good humor. He might as well have been a million miles from Moscow, so remote was he from the power struggle that was casting a growing shadow in the Kremlin.

In the fall he began to receive visitors. Although he was still unable to speak much, it was clear from the few words he could pronounce clearly that he understood what was being said. Even political interest was returning, for on several occasions he listened intently as Party officials came to Gorki to report on the latest developments.

When the snows came, the Gorki estate lay under a coat of ermine white. It was very much like the winters of his boyhood. Lenin loved to gaze out of the window at the quiet splendor of the countryside, his features relaxed in peaceful contentment.

At Christmastime, Nadezhda and his sister Maria ordered a fir tree cut down and had it set up in the sprawling living room. The tree was decorated with candles; presents were heaped under it. Children from the village of Gorki were invited in for a party. They danced around the tree and opened their gifts with squeals of joy. When Lenin limped in on his cane, they swarmed all over him and sat on his lap.

With each day his mental faculties seemed to improve. Nadezhda read to him daily, particularly from the works of the American author Jack London, for whom Lenin had developed a great affection.

In the middle of January, the Thirteenth Communist Party Congress opened in Moscow. Lenin, of course, was unable to attend. Trotsky, too, was absent, having been laid low by an ailment which the doctors were still unable to diagnose.

With Lenin and Trotsky both indisposed, Stalin judged that it was the right moment to make an open bid for power. He had already paved the way for such a move by having enough of his supporters appointed as delegates to the Congress to dominate its sessions.

From this point on, the Congress was stage-managed by Stalin as shrewdly as Party meetings used to be manipulated by Lenin in the old days. When Stalin got up to speak, his remarks were carefully calculated to achieve the precise objective he had in mind. Of Lenin, he spoke almost deferentially, for the ailing Lenin was too respected as the elder statesman of the Party to be vulnerable to attack. Trotsky, however, did not have Lenin's stature. Stalin proceeded to unleash a vitriolic attack on the absent official. He accused Trotsky of crimes against the Communist Party, including high treason. He charged that Trotsky had encouraged students and intellectuals to oppose the views of the Party's "Old Guard."

"Trotsky's error," shouted Stalin, "lies in the fact that he has elevated himself into a superman standing above the Central Committee, above its laws and above its decisions, and in this way he has provided certain groups within the Party with a pretext for undermining confidence in the Central Committee."

For three days Stalin continued his attack on Trotsky, both in public and behind closed doors at private caucuses. He related exaggerated stories of Trotsky's alleged insulting and insubordinate behavior. The few delegates who sought to defend Trotsky were quickly intimidated by threats from Stalin and his followers. When the Congress adjourned on January 18, it was clear that Stalin had won his bid for power. He had managed to impose his will on the entire Communist Party. Thus, he was now the undisputed master of the Party and of Soviet Russia.

At Gorki, the seemingly indestructible Lenin remained isolated from the political winds that were blowing in Moscow. He read about the events at the Thirteenth Congress in the papers and was undoubtedly dismayed by them. However, the bad news was partially offset by encouraging reports from his physicians. They predicted a full recovery, promising him that he would be back to work by summer!

On the night of January 20 Lenin went to bed in better-than-usual spirits. In the morning, he seemed the same except that he refused breakfast. As the day wore on, Nadezhda and Maria noticed that he seemed increasingly listless; but they were not worried, for they attributed his mood to the weather, which was cold and depressing. Throughout the afternoon, he slept or dozed. Then at

Epilogue

WITH THE EMERGENCE of Joseph Stalin as the undisputed dictator of the Soviet Union, Leon Trotsky was driven into exile. In 1940, he was murdered in Mexico by an assassin assumed to be an agent of the Russian secret police.

Stalin reigned as the absolute ruler of Russia for thirty years, until his death in 1953. During that time, his ceaseless efforts to maintain himself in power by eliminating his enemies, real and imagined, resulted in the death of millions of Russians. The ruthless despotism begun under Lenin thus ran its full course under Stalin, matching the cruelest excesses of the tsarist autocracy.

The Russian Revolution marked the beginning of an era of international social and political upheaval that saw the spread of Communism to every corner of the earth. It was a movement that fed on human misery by exploiting poverty and despair. During the three decades following the revolution of 1917, more than a billion people came under a Russian-dominated Communist hegemony. By the late 1950's, however, Russia's hold over the rest of the Communist world began to weaken. The world moved further and further from Lenin's original dream of a united international Communist order—the dream that had been the ultimate objective of his revolution.

nightfall his breathing became irregular. A physician, Dr. Foerster, was summoned.

A few minutes later, Lenin began to breathe in heavy, labored gasps. Soon he went into convulsions, and his temperature soared frighteningly. Dr. Foerster shook his head despairingly. There was little he could do. The convulsions grew so intense that Lenin's wracked body was hurled from one side of the bed to the other. The labored breathing then became intermittent. Finally, it stopped altogether.

Vladimir I. Lenin, fifty-four, was pronounced dead on the evening of January 21, 1924.

Two days later, Lenin's body was carried in a red coffin by railroad train from Gorki to Moscow. All along the twenty-mile route great crowds lined the tracks.

The sky was leaden and snow was falling when the train lumbered into the Moscow station. The coffin was removed and borne on the shoulders of pallbearers for nearly five miles along the wind- and snow-swept streets. Hundreds of thousands of people crowded the sidewalks to pay their last respects and to catch a glimpse of Lenin's lifeless face as he lay in the open crimson coffin.

For nearly a week the body lay in state in the House of Trade Unions where mourners by the tens of thousands filed past. On Sunday, January 27, it was transferred to a wooden vault in Red Square, near the Kremlin itself. (In later years the wooden structure would be replaced by a magnificent granite mausoleum, and the embalmed body would be re-treated by a special process for permanent preservation.)

At exactly four o'clock that Sunday, all over Russia, every device capable of making noise was turned on in honor of the man who had led the Communist revolution. Sirens, steam whistles, foghorns and bells joined together across the vast land for three minutes of tribute. They were assisted by the roar of cannon at army garrisons and the massive guns from the ships of the Soviet fleet. Perhaps never before in the history of the world had there been such an explosion of sound. It seemed to symbolize the upheaval taking place in Russia itself—one that would be felt for years to come.

Bibliography

Abramovitch, Raphael R. *The Soviet Revolution.* New York: International Universities Press, 1962.
Berlin, Isaiah. *Karl Marx.* New York: Oxford University Press, 1963.
Carr, E. H. *A History of Soviet Russia.* New York: The Macmillan Company, 1951.
Clarkson, Jesse D. *A History of Russia.* New York: Random House, 1961.
Fischer, Louis. *The Life of Lenin.* New York: Harper & Row Publishers, 1964.
Fotieva, Lydia. *Pages from Lenin's Life.* Moscow: Foreign Languages Publishing House, 1960.
Gruber, Helmut. *International Communism in the Era of Lenin: A Documentary History.* New York: Fawcett Publications, Inc., 1967.
Kennan, George F. *Russia and the West.* Boston and Toronto: Little, Brown & Company, 1961.
Kerensky, A. F. *The Crucifixion of Liberty.* New York: John Day, 1934.
Moorehead, Alan. *The Russian Revolution.* New York: Harper & Row Publishers, 1958.
Payne, Robert. *The Life and Death of Lenin.* New York: Simon & Schuster, 1964.
Reed, John. *Ten Days That Shook the World.* New York: Random House, 1960.
Shub, David. *Lenin.* New York: Doubleday & Co., 1950.
Thayer, Charles W. *Russia.* New York: Time, Inc., 1963.
Thomson, David. *Europe Since Napoleon.* New York: Alfred A. Knopf, 1957.

Trotsky, Leon.   *Lenin.* New York: Grosset & Dunlap, 1960.
——— *My Life.* New York: Charles Scribner's Sons, 1930.
——— *The Russian Revolution.* Garden City, New York: Doubleday & Co., 1959.
Wilson, Edmund.   *To the Finland Station.* New York: Doubleday & Company, 1940.
Wolfe, Bertram D.   *Marxism.* New York: The Dial Press, 1965.
——— *Three Who Made a Revolution.* New York: The Dial Press, 1948.
Wren, Melvin.   *The Course of Russian History.* New York: The Macmillan Company, 1963.

Index

Alexander I, 32
Alexander II, 20-22, 23, 24, 30, 33
Alexander III, 23-24, 26, 29, 33, 34, 36, 64, 65
Arefyev, 54
Armand, Elisabeth, 109-110, 111, 116, 128
Assembly of Russian Factory and Mill Workers, See Russia, labor union movement
Astrakhan, 9, 14
Axelrod, Paul, 61, 62, 65, 80, 88, 90

Batu, 15
Bestuzhevka, 54
Black Hundreds, 100-101
Black Sea, 19
Bloody Sunday (January 22, 1905), 94-95, 96
Bolsheviks, 89, 97, 102, 104, 108, 110-113, 124, 131, 132, 135, 140-142, 143, 144-146, 152, 153-159, 160, 161

boyars, 17
Brest-Litovsk Treaty, See Russia, Treaty of Brest-Litovsk
Bronstein, Lev Davydovich, See Trotsky, Leon
Bubnov, Andrey, 144
Bund, The, See Jewish Socialist Bund

Capital, 22, 45, 46-47
Caspian Sea, 9, 14, 16
Catherine the Great, 18, 31
Cheka, 154, 158, 162, 164, 165, 169, 170
Chernov, Victor, 156, 157
Chkeidze, Nikolay, 132
Committee of Salvation, 152
Committee on Literacy, 59, 60
Communism, 33, 46-48, 59, 82
Communist League, 33
Communist Manifesto, 33, 82, 88
Constantine, 32
Constituent Assembly, 154-158
Cossacks, 31

Decembrists, *See* Russia, Decembrist Uprising
Development of Capitalism in Russia, The, 72, 81, 86
Djugashvili, Joseph, *See* Stalin, Joseph
Duma, *See* National Duma

Elisarov, Mark, 42, 45, 49, 54, 69
Engels, Friedrich, 33, 75, 82, 139, 167
Essen, Maria, 91

Finland Station, 131
Forward, The, See Vperyod
Franz Joseph, Emperor, 113, 114

Gapon, Father George, 93, 94, 95, 100
Genghis Khan, 15
Gil, Stepan, 164
Gorky, Maxim, 105, 110

Igor, 14
Iskra, 78, 79, 80, 81, 82, 83, 84, 85, 86, 90, 91
Ivan I, 15-16
Ivan the Terrible, 16

Japan, 92
Jewish Socialist Bund, 87-88, 89

Kalita, Ivan, *See* Ivan I
Kalmykova, 78
Kamenev, Lev, 112, 113, 144, 176
Kaplan, Fanya, 165, 167
Kashkadamova, Vera, 29
Kautsky, Karl, 116
Kazan, 11, 14; University of, 38, 39, 40, 41

Kerensky, Alexander, 121, 123, 126, 134, 136, 137, 141, 144, 145, 146, 147, 149, 152
Kerensky, Feodor, 38
Kiev, 14, 15
Kokushkino, 39, 42, 49
Khandin, Andrey, 51, 52, 54
Kornilov, General Lavr, 137-138, 141
Kranoyarsk, 69, 70, 76
Krupskaya, Nadezhda Konstantinovna, 58, 59, 60, 61, 64, 66, 67, 68, 72, 73, 76, 91, 110, 166, 176-177

Lenin (Ulyanov, Vladimir Ilyich), childhood in Simbirsk, 10-13, 20-22, 25-28; early religious beliefs, 22; death of father, 27-28; brother executed, 37; accepted to University of Kazan, 38; becomes law student, 40; arrested, 41; retires to family estate, 42-45; discovers Marxism, 45-48; becomes a lawyer, 53; early political activity, 55-56; moves to St. Petersburg, 56; travels abroad, 61-63; arrested in St. Petersburg, 66-68; exiled to Siberia, 68-77; marries, 73-74; develops ideas on revolution, 75, 82, 139-140; editor of *Iskra,* 77-78, 80-82, 90; political activities abroad, 79-86, 87-97, 104-105, 108-110; attends Party Congress in Brussels, 87-89; formation of Bolshevik party, 87-89; establishes school for revolutionaries, 110-111; refuses to support Russia in war, 115-117; mother dies,

INDEX

116-117; attitude towards provisional government, 126-127, 133, 142; boards sealed German train, 128-130; returns to Russia, 130-133; denounced as German spy, 135-136; convinces Central Committee to endorse armed uprising, 142-144; addresses Second Congress of Soviets, 151; organizes defense of Petrograd, 152-153; consolidates Bolshevik power, 154-155, 161; seeks peace with Germany, 159-161; shot, 164-165; administers government, 167-170; ill health, 171-180; denounces Stalin, 175; death, 180
London, 84
Luch, 111
Lvov, Prince, 134, 136, 137

Malinovsky, Roman, 111, 112, 113
Manchuria, 92, 97
Martov, Jules, 78, 80, 85, 88, 89, 90, 125
Marx, Karl, 23, 33, 45-48, 51, 53, 58, 59, 60, 75, 82, 88
Marxism, 59, 60, 61, 82, 175
Materialism and Empirio-Criticism, 109
Mensheviks, 89, 90, 96, 99, 101, 102, 104, 108, 110-113, 133, 134, 152
Mikhailov, Dr., 67
Minsk, 72, 87
Mir, 21, 24
Mongols, *See* Tartars
Moscow, 13, 15, 57, 69
Moskovskaya Street, 28, 37

Napoleon, 31
Narodnaya Volya, 20
National Duma, 96, 100, 103-104, 105, 110, 120, 121, 122, 123
New Economic Policy, 169, 170
Nicholas II, Tsar, 64, 93, 94, 95, 96, 100, 101, 103, 105, 119, 122-124, 163

Obolensky, Prince, 77
October Manifesto, 100, 101
Oleg, 14
Okhrana, 20

Pestel, Colonel Paul, 32, 33
Peter III, 18, 19, 31
Peter the Great, 17-18
Petrograd, *See* St. Petersburg
Plekhanov, George, 61, 62, 65, 78, 79, 80, 85, 86, 87, 88, 89, 90, 115, 133, 135, 136
Poland, 19
Port Arthur, 92
Potemkin, *See* Russia, Potemkin mutiny
Potresov, Alexander, 78, 90
Pravda, 111, 112, 126
Princip, Gavril, 114
Pskov, 77
Pugachev, Emilian, 31

Rasputin, Gregory, 106-107, 119-121
Red Guard, 141, 153
Revolution of 1905, *See* Russia, Revolution of 1905
Roosevelt, Theodore, 97
Rovio, Gustav, 138
Rurik, 14

Russia, 13; early history, 14-19; cultural heritage, 16; westernization, 17-19; emancipation of serfs, 21-24; reign of Alexander III, 23-24; Pugachev's rebellion, 31; Decembrist uprising, 32-33; Nicholas II comes to throne, 64-65; Russo-Japanese war, 92-93, 94, 96, 97; labor union movement, 93-95; Potemkin mutiny, 96-97; October reforms (1905), 100-101; Revolution of 1905, 100-105; war breaks out, 113-114; military defeat, 118-121; March Revolution, 121-125; Nicholas abdicates, 123; Provisional Government formed, 123-124, 125, 126-127; Kornilov plot, 137-138, 141; Bolsheviks increase power, 140-142, 144; November Revolution, 145-158; Treaty of Brest-Litovsk, 159-161; The White Armies attack, 161-163, 164, 166; royal family executed, 164

Russian Academy of Sciences, 17

St. Petersburg, 13, 17, 18, 34, 36, 37, 53, 56, 57, 63, 65, 93, 94, 99, 100, 152; University of, 25, 30
St. Vladimir, 9
Samara, 49, 51, 55, 56
Scandinavians, 14
Shevyrev, Pyotr, 33
Siberia, 16, 32, 68-77
Simbirsk, 10, 12, 28, 37, 38, 39
Social Democratic Party, 72, 75, 81, 86, 108, 110; 2nd Congress, 87-89; 5th Congress, 104

Social Revolutionary Party, 72, 165
Socialism, 33, 45
Solkolnikov, Grigory, 144
Soviets, 99, 100
Spark, The, See Iskra
Stalin, Joseph, 104, 108, 112, 113, 133, 144, 152, 171, 172-174, 175-178, 179-180, 182
State and Revolution, The, 139
Sukhanov, Nikolay, 143
Sushenskoye, 70, 71, 73
Sverdlov, Jacob, 112, 113

Tannenberg, Battle of, 118
Tartars, 9, 14, 15, 16
Tolstoy, Leo, 55
Treaty of Portsmouth (September 1905), 97
Trotsky, Leon, 85-86, 88, 89, 90, 97, 99, 100, 101, 104, 133, 140, 144, 145-148, 150, 152, 153, 157, 158, 159-160, 166, 171, 173, 174, 177, 179, 180, 182

Ufa, 73, 76
Ulyanov, Alexander (brother), 11, 12, 22-23, 24, 26, 28; arrested, 29-31, 33, 34-36; tried for assassination attempt, 36; executed, 37
Ulyanov, Anna (sister), 25, 27, 28, 29, 33, 37, 39, 42, 44, 45
Ulyanov, Dmitry (brother), 11, 57, 79
Ulyanov, Ilya Nikolaevich (father), 9-11, 13, 22, 25-27, 40
Ulyanov, Maria (sister), 11, 57, 79

INDEX

Ulyanov, Maria Alexandrovna (mother), 9, 10-11, 22, 25, 27, 35, 36, 37, 39, 48, 49, 50, 51, 52, 79
Ulyanov, Olga (sister), 11, 53
Ulyanov, Vladimir Ilyich, *See* Lenin
Union of Soviet Socialist Republics, *See* Russia
Ural Mountains, 70
Uritsky, Moses, 154, 164, 165

Valday Hills, 13
Vienna, 15
Vladimir (king), 14
Vladivostok, 92
Volga, 9, 10, 11, 13-14, 54, 55

Volkenstein, M. F., 57
Vorontsov, Vasily, 57, 58, 62
Vperyod, 91, 92, 93, 95, 98

What's to be Done? 82-84, 88, 99
Witte, Count Sergei, 105
Worker's Cause, The, 66
World War I, 113-116

Yaroslav (king), 14
Yenisei River, 70, 76

Zasulich, Vera, 78, 80, 85, 90
Zemstvos, 24
Zinoviev, Grigory, 144, 176
Zyrianov, Apollon, 71

About the Author

I. E. LEVINE is a native New Yorker. He graduated from DeWitt Clinton High School and enrolled at the City College of New York as a physics major. After working on the college newspaper for two years, he was convinced that he wanted to be a writer and changed his major to English and the social sciences. He received his degree, went to work in the public relations department at City College, and in 1954 was appointed to his present post of Director of Public Relations. He has written many articles for national magazines, is co-author of several adult books and well known for his biographies for young people. He and his family make their home in Kew Gardens Hills, Long Island.